Claiming
All Things
for God

Claiming All Things for God

Prayer, Discernment,
and Ritual for Social Change

GEORGE D. MCCLAIN

Abingdon Press
Nashville

CLAIMING ALL THINGS FOR GOD
PRAYER, DISCERNMENT, AND RITUAL FOR SOCIAL CHANGE

Copyright © 1998 by Abingdon Press

This book is printed on recycled, acid-free paper.

Library of Congress Cataloging-in-Publication Data

McClain, George D., 1938-
    Claiming all things for God : prayer, discernment and ritual for social change / George D. McClain.
        p.   cm.
    Includes bibliographical references.
    ISBN 0-687-00489-6 (pbk. : alk. paper)
    1. Prayer.   2. Church and the world.   3. Social action.   4. Church and social problems.
5. Prayers.   6. Ritual.   I. Title.
BV227.M33   1998
248.3'2—dc21   97-50249
                                                                                    CIP

98 99 00 01 02 03 04 05 06 07—10 9 8 7 6 5 4 3 2 1

MANUFACTURED IN THE UNITED STATES OF AMERICA

To Tilda, Noah, and Shana,
through whom I have received so
richly of God's gifts and goodness

Contents

List of Prayer Forms

Foreword

by

W a l t e r

W i n k

The greatest religious challenge of our age is to hold together social action and spiritual disciplines. This is not just a theological necessity, dictated by the need to integrate all of life around the reality of the living God. It is a matter of sheer survival. The evils we confront are so massive, so inhuman, so impervious to appeals and dead to compassion, that those who struggle against them face the real possibility of being overcome by them.

The dangers are legion. Social activists who have not excavated their shadow side may be projecting their own inner cesspool onto the enemy. In such cases, the struggle for justice is contaminated by a desire for revenge, or a need to feel righteous (coming out of a deep conviction that we are not). We may find ourselves involved in activism in order to feel good about ourselves, on the theory that if we are *doing* good we must *be* good. Or we may simply burn out, having thrown ourselves against the barricades one time too many for our spiritual stamina to sustain. And so we lapse into inactivity, withdraw from the struggle, go off to India in search of a guru, take up ballroom dancing, or whatever, as we attempt to heal from the ravages of social struggle.

George McClain did a survey of the national board members of the church-related social action network with which he works. When asked how their chapter tended to frame its decision making on a spectrum of "What are we going to do?" on one end and "What is

God's yearning for us?" on the other, the *chapters'* way of making decisions was close to the end of the spectrum representing the question "What shall we do?" But when asked how these same social action leaders handle their own personal decision making, their average response was almost exactly as far on the opposite end of the spectrum. This survey exposes our profound inability to act in concert with others out of the deepest sources of our tradition. Instead, we work from the lowest common denominator, so as not to offend anyone who might not share our deeply personal beliefs.

This was the error we made repeatedly during the resistance to the Vietnam War. Jews and Christians would come together, never to worship, never to pray, but simply to march, bearing our symbols, dressed in our robes, but unable to *be* religious together.

Some of us learned from that. In the crises that followed, we began to ask the rabbis among us to lead us in Jewish worship. We asked the Pentecostals to do the same. We began to live out of our traditions instead of suppressing them. But McClain's survey shows that we still have a long way to go. Social action is something *we* do. God scarcely gets a nod.

This book can solve that problem. It not only provides a superb analysis of our need, but it actually provides rituals that we can use straight off the page, or jump off from into our own creative liturgies. McClain has done his spiritual work, and is in a position to help the rest of us do so. This book is a manual for survival in the face of towering evil. It arms us to struggle with the Powers on behalf of the humanizing purposes of God. This is theology at its best: practical, prophetic, and profound.

Preface

Although I have deeply yearned, throughout my nearly forty years as a Christian social activist, for a more complete sense of integration between action and spiritual life, it has been slow in coming. I took an important first step in the current phase of my journey when I enrolled in a training program for spiritual directors, not really knowing what spiritual direction was. In the inner dialogue between that course and my work with the Methodist Federation for Social Action, these two parts of my life were joined as never before. Soon I found myself united with others in an intensive prayer-action enterprise, especially in the struggle to gain our denomination's support for economic sanctions against the apartheid regime in South Africa.

I seek here to explore and develop some of the implications of these and related experiences. On one level, it is a very personal undertaking, part of my working out my own "salvation with fear and trembling" (Philippians 2:12). But it is also a community project, building upon the growing intersection in people's lives of action for justice and the inner journey in the Spirit.

I want to stress that the context within which I write is the predominantly white, mostly middle-class Protestant church in the United States. The analyses, issues, and prescriptions for other contexts need to arise from within those communities.

Along the way I have received the blessings of association with many communities. The Methodist Federation for Social Action, which I have had the privilege of staffing for twenty-five years, has been like a large family to me, and many of its members have been an intimate and indispensable part of this journey. The training experiences I have had with the Center for Spirituality and Justice, Bronx, New York, and the Shalem Institute for Spiritual Formation, Washington, D.C., have led me through new spiritual frontiers. The Methodist Federation for Social Action provided me with the opportunity and encouragement to pursue this project, and the personal participation of many has been indispensable. My colleagues in the Prayer House Community have walked with me in very special ways.

The other community that has been so important is a unique institution, New York Theological Seminary. I am especially grateful for the mentoring of Dr. T. Richard Snyder, dean of graduate programs, and Dr. Norman K. Gottwald, my advisor. Over a period of three years, members of my Doctor of Ministry site team took time from their very busy schedules to travel considerable distances, in some cases hundreds of miles, to reflect with me. They include Martha Cline, John Collins, Randy Day, Jane Eesley, Lee MacCallum, Jane Middleton, Marty Morrison, Kate Parker-Burgard, Carolyn Watson, and Odella Williamson. They have been helpful and gentle critics, as well as active and faithful participants in this project.

I am deeply grateful to Diane Large for her incomparable assistance in word processing this manuscript. Her diligence, skill, and good spirit, even under trying circumstances, have been a great blessing.

I owe a special debt of gratitude to my best friend and spouse, Tilda Norberg, whose ministry of healing has stimulated my development and ideas in so many ways and whose personal care and support have been beyond measure.

Chapter

Spiritual Practice and Social Action:

Signs of a New Partnership

To divide contemplation from prophecy is to damage and maybe destroy both.
Kenneth Leech

The previous year's church convention had been very contentious and negative. The gymnasium-turned-conference hall had been more a place of competition, of winning and losing, than a place of the church in conference. And since that previous meeting, discordant voices were being raised to champion "godly patriarchy" in a regional church body that prided itself on the great strides it had made toward partnership between men and women, laity and clergy.

Seeking to be an instrument of God's healing, a social action group within the church judicatory brought together a small band of persons to pray early each morning during the following year's convention. Each person was assigned a different area of the gymnasium to focus on. Then together they spoke prayers to cleanse the conference of alien principalities and powers:

REMOVE FROM THIS SPACE ANY SPIRIT OF WORLDLY AMBITION AND COMPETITION.
REMOVE FROM THIS SPACE THE POWERS OF CLOSED-MINDEDNESS THAT KEEP YOUR FAITHFUL FROM HEARING ONE ANOTHER.
REMOVE FROM THIS SPACE THE POWER OF FEAR THAT KEEPS FAITHFUL CHRISTIANS FROM DARING TO BE BRAVE AND TRUE TO THE GOSPEL OF LOVE AS GIVEN TO US BY CHRIST JESUS.
REMOVE FROM THIS SPACE ALL THE

POWERS AND PRINCIPALITIES THAT PREVENT THE GATHERED
CHURCH FROM BEING THE TRUE BODY OF CHRIST, IN MINISTRY
TO ONE ANOTHER AND TO ALL THE WORLD, IN THE SPIRIT OF JUS-
TICE, RIGHTEOUSNESS, AND LOVE.

Then, in a positive vein, the group claimed the space for the Reign
of God, sharing in the well-known prayer for the church by Social
Gospel theologian Walter Rauschenbusch: "O God of all times and
places, we pray for your church, which is set today amid the per-
plexities of a changing order.... Help us to proclaim boldly the
coming of your kingdom."

The service, a creative adaptation of the denominational service
for consecration of a church building, was advertised in a daily news
sheet and by word of mouth. Everyone was invited to join in this
cleansing service each morning of the conference. Interestingly, one
morning two hearing-impaired persons participated, together with
their signer; thus, the cleansing and claiming prayers were enacted
in sign language as well as spoken language.

When I asked Diane, the pastor who created and led the services,
what difference these prayers made, she replied:

We felt we did what we could to bring about the exorcism of
those principalities and powers. It did feel like a "cleaner" space
and we felt "cleaner" inside too. One person said it made her
tingle to read these "removes." As for the conference as a
whole, who knows? But it is true that we were in a whole different mood this year, and the high point of the conference was
the bishop's initial remarks, which set a very different tone from
the previous year, including his positive remarks about women
and theology—including Sophia.

Such an instance of social action prayer is by no means typical of
American church life, at least in the mainline, predominantly white
churches with which I am familiar. But neither is it an isolated example. Consider these instances:

• After thirty Ku Klux Klansmen held a rally on the courthouse
steps in Fort Wayne, Indiana, one hundred Christians con-

cerned about racism and violence gathered the next day at precisely the same spot for a prayer service to repudiate the spiritual violence done there by the Klan and to reclaim that space for God. Holy water was sprinkled "to reclaim that ground as holy ground," explained one of the organizers. As a witness against violence, the group pledged to hold similar services at the sites of murders in the city.

- An interfaith candlelight vigil at the Arkansas governor's mansion and at Cummins Prison protested the "legalized violence" of the death penalty and the record-breaking execution of three men within a span of two and a half hours.

- On special Sundays when major rallies or marches for justice are held in Washington, D.C., or Baltimore, Maryland, a congregation in Baltimore frequently adjourns its regular Sunday worship to reconvene at the site of the rally for Eucharist and prayer before participating in the event.

- San Francisco Bay area social activists gather for an annual Good Friday vigil at the Livermore Laboratories, site of extensive weapons research. The area United Methodist bishop traditionally participates and has, on occasion, been among those arrested in nonviolent civil disobedience protest witness.

- Connecticut area clergy and laity joined striking workers from an electronics company in a candlelight worship service and "social exorcism" in front of the home of the company's owner.

- Minnesota Christian activists have been holding a protest prayer vigil at the Prairie Island nuclear waste storage site.

- Chicago social activists have staged a prayer witness as part of an abortion clinic defense.

- Colorado activists held a candlelight prayer vigil of protest when that state approved an amendment to the state constitution overturning local gay rights laws.

- Some seventy-five Christians have been gathering in a Cleveland area church every three months for a service of repentance for their denomination's stance on homosexuality.

Such examples represent the public side of a growing movement to unite the works of piety and the works of social justice, arenas which, at least in the white community, have long been worlds apart.

A Pastoral Concern

For generations we Christian social activists have not drunk as deeply as we might have from the wells of spiritual nurture. But a shift is taking place, and there is evidence of a widespread desire today for bringing these worlds together. Weighed down by the burdens we bear, many of us are realizing that we simply cannot do without this living water.

As Christian activists, we bear the mark of those called to witness to the reality and presence of what Jesus called the Reign of God—a way of peace, justice, partnership, and egalitarianism. We are an extension of Jesus' original community, a "discipleship of equals" in theologian Elisabeth Schüssler-Fiorenza's words, called into existence as exemplars and heralds of this in-breaking Reign of God.

As part of this community, we bear an aching and sometimes wearying burden of living, witnessing, and acting against principalities and powers of evil. Seeking to be faithful to God as known in Jesus Christ, we often find ourselves on the prophetic edge, vulnerable, exposed, and not always knowing how to "sing God's song in a foreign land" (Psalm 137:4). Symbolic of the isolated context of so many Christian social activists is the pastor in a small town in northeastern Ohio who some years back, when the local results of a presidential primary were published, knew without a doubt that the only two votes for Jesse Jackson were those of him and his wife. In such vulnerable and isolated situations—whether in local congregations, workplaces, families, academic settings, or community groups—we carry a special weight and manifest a particular vulnerability to burnout, overwork, despair, and loneliness, even as we seek to bear the good news of God's in-breaking Reign.

My conclusion is that numerous activists, myself included, as well as our social action networks, are impoverished by our insufficient attention to the grounding, sustenance, nurture, and empowerment available to us in our relation to God. Tilden Edwards, founder of the Shalem Institute for Spiritual Formation, says it well:

> If such action [for peace and justice] is to be sustained and discerning, it must be rooted in a direct relation to God in prayer, Scripture, and daily attentiveness, not only for the activist, but as part of the goal for the community for whom he or she works. Without a deep spiritual vision, realism about grace and freedom, and sustained discipline, no community can have an adequate foundation for the fullness of life to which we are called. It is hard enough to find our way *with* these. Without them, we lose our orientation to the discerning knowledge of how to be in the world but not of it: alone and together.[1]

I rejoice, therefore, in this particular time of new possibility for a growing integration of spiritual practice and social advocacy. I believe we are moving into a new era for living lives which integrate the spiritual and the social, the active and the contemplative.

Challenges to Overcome

This increasing unity of the active and the contemplative, however, must make its way despite significant resistance. To begin, the dominant culture in which we live has been uncomfortable with public expression of sincere religious faith and practice, especially prophetic expression. In standard television, for instance, positive images of religious practice have been hard to find. When clergy have been portrayed, they have usually appeared in caricature form, exemplifying rigidity, moralism, and hypocrisy. Even as there have been signs of a shift in network attitudes toward religious practice, television programming of the last several years has stopped short of depicting the encounter with transcendent reality.

In the beautiful film *Shadowlands*, based on a special episode in the life of the widely acclaimed Christian writer C. S. Lewis, the last words of his dying wife to him are, "You have made me happy." But unreported was her final faith testimony to her chaplain, "I am at peace with God."

A remarkable example of blindness to life-shaping religious prac-tice is found in Taylor Branch's otherwise outstanding chronicle of Dr. Martin Luther King, Jr. and the Civil Rights movement. There can be no doubt that King preached and lived out of a deep Christian faith. Yet in all of Branch's monumental volume of 1,064 pages, King's life of prayer is treated in less than half a page, and in that dis-cussion the word "God" is avoided altogether.

The secularity of the dominant culture has made inroads into the church as well. In a recent church survey, leaders of a major main-line denomination were asked to rank in order the qualities they sought in a pastor. Of the fifteen qualities listed, "spiritual leader-ship" ranked a low seventh, well below preaching, management/administration, pastoral care, biblical knowledge, leadership/vision-ing, and communication skills.

History, ideology, worldview, and custom work to keep spiritual practice and social action separated. Even those who intend for them to be united experience difficulty. Coordinators for a denomination-wide network of "covenant discipleship" groups, a program of vol-untary small groups for mutual accountability in local churches and seminaries, report that of the four areas of accountability—works of piety, works of mercy, works of justice, and corporate worship—the one area in which groups have a really difficult time developing a meaningful covenant is works of justice.

When I surveyed the leaders of the regional units of the denomi-national social action group I serve, fewer than half of those responding to a survey could report any instances in which their group included prayer or worship as part of the group's social wit-ness. Hardly any had a tradition of a regular spiritual retreat. While most scheduled an overnight gathering from time to time, which they termed a "retreat," the content of the meeting was usually an exploration of a social issue or a planning time for future activities, rather than a retreat with a spiritual focus.

I also asked these leaders about their personal devotional prac-tices. The comparison was striking. The level of "frequent" or "rather often" personal participation was higher for every form of spiritual practice about which I asked, and strikingly higher in regard to spiritual life retreat, Bible study, Eucharist, contemplative prayer, and spiritual discernment.

Although not a scientific study, this informal survey does suggest what other evidence corroborates. Social activist Christians are not without a devotional life, nor without attention to the traditional means of grace in prayer and Christian ritual. However, our personal devotional life as activists is significantly richer than our corporate devotional life as activist groups.

For whatever reason, we lack the habits and forms of devotional life—as action groups—through which to share in prayer, ritual, discernment, sacrament, and spiritual retreat. Such spiritual practice appears to be lacking both in our intentional group life and in our more public social action witness. If, as Kenneth Leech maintains, "True spirituality... is essentially subversive," then we may be missing something critical.

Reclaiming the Tradition of Moses

"So come, I will send you to Pharaoh to bring my people, the Israelites, out of Egypt". Exodus 3:10

In spite of the substantial resistance to the effective uniting of prayer and action, there is a general movement of spiritual awakening which is creating new possibilities for this unity. Many commentators speak of a new interest in spirituality over the last several decades. Speaking from a German perspective, Gerhard Wehr contends that "the signs of the times are unmistakable."[2] There is renewed reflection on the great traditions of Christian spirituality, he says, and religious experience has "gained new respect."

An Anglican commentator observes that "more people than ever before are exploring methods of wordless prayer and contemplation, acknowledging the importance of bodily posture, seeking God in silence and simplicity."[3]

In North America, too, there is a surge of interest in spirituality. According to Gerald May, "Historians of the future will probably look back upon the 1970's as a time of spiritual reawakening in America."[4] The continuing increase of interest in spirituality has been remarkable. Workplace prayer groups, Torah classes, and Islamic study groups are proliferating. Spiritual formation, once a traditional Roman Catholic emphasis, is now widely practiced by Protestants. Seminary course offerings, training programs, and spiritual retreats are on the increase, often taking place, ironically, in Roman Catholic facilities which have come to depend upon considerable use by Protestants.

At the same time, there are many signs of deep dissatisfaction among activists regarding the deep chasm between the spiritual life and the advocacy of justice. Just a few months before it was suddenly announced that the venerable social action journal *Christianity and Crisis* would cease publication, a clergy colleague, quite sympathetic to the journal's perspective on issues, commented, "People are dropping *Christianity and Crisis* because there seems to be more crisis than Christianity." Speaking of spirituality and action, she said, "I don't have energy for one without the other. Alone, each is flat." A pastor in Baltimore complains, "We force into being instead of pray into being." "We work ourselves to death as if we have to do it all," laments an inner-city pastor from Philadelphia.

There is a growing sense among church activists that while spiritual life apart from a deep caring for basic justice concerns is bankrupt, social advocacy without deep spiritual grounding is also deeply lacking. We are discovering that holding spiritual life and justice advocacy apart is a violation of our Judeo-Christian faith. We are reclaiming the Moses tradition which is so central to our faith story.

According to the Exodus tradition, Moses, though raised among Egyptian royalty, is forced into exile because he killed an Egyptian who was beating one of his Hebrew kinsfolk. While tending his Midianite father-in-law's sheep, Moses comes to Horeb, the mountain of God. There the messenger of God appears to Moses in a blazing bush. Moses hears God call his name out of the bush and instructs him to remove his shoes "for the place on which you are standing is holy ground" (Exodus 3:5). God appears as the God of his people's ancestors, and Moses hides his face because he is "afraid to look at God" (Exodus 3:6).

Unfortunately, this awesome text, for all practical purposes, ends here for many of us; we treat what follows as a separate text. But note how the luminous mystery of God's self-revelation to Moses actually embraces a staggering injunction to be God's instrument of divine liberation. Still speaking from the bush, God commissions Moses to lead the Israelites out of slavery:

I have observed the misery of my people who are in Egypt; I have heard their cry on account of their taskmasters. Indeed, I know their sufferings, and I have come down to deliver them from the Egyptians, and to bring them up out of that land to a good and broad land, a land flowing with milk and honey, to the country of the Canaanites, the Hittites, the Amorites, the Perizzites, the Hivites, and the Jebusites. The cry of the Israelites has now come to me; I have also seen how the Egyptians oppress them. So come, I will send you to Pharaoh to bring my people, the Israelites, out of Egypt. (Exodus 3:7-10)

The preacher or teacher who emphasizes the spiritual relationship to God may be tempted to stop at the point where Moses hides his face and to focus on Moses' naked, almost empty experience of the Holy and on the cultivation of such mountaintop experiences of God's presence. On the other hand, the preacher or teacher who emphasizes doing justice faces the opposite temptation. He or she may well skip lightly over the burning bush theophany in order to focus on the powerful subsequent text in which Yahweh reveals intimate knowledge and deep empathy for the tearful sufferings of the oppressed Hebrews in Egypt, declares the intention to deliver them from the clutches of slavery, and directs this startled Moses to go to the hated, feared Pharaoh and lead the Israelites out of Egypt.

Yet we dare neglect neither portion of the text. If social activists comprehend that Moses' call to be a liberator arises as a constituent part of an overpowering personal experience of the holy, transcendent presence of God—so overpowering that he must hide his face, so very personal that he hears himself called by his very own name, and so awesome that he removes his shoes in reverence—they cannot any longer demean personal religious experience or the cultivation of openness to the holy. And if the cultivators of religious experience comprehend that the content of Moses' overwhelming experience of the divine presence is precisely to be liberator of his people from slavery, they will no longer cultivate piety apart from pursuing justice.

The mystical-prophetic summons comes to sensitive persons in our era as in that of Moses, sometimes in ways that echo biblical accounts in remarkable fashion. A longtime social activist tells how, during his student days, he once knelt at a communion rail and audibly, clearly heard a voice he knew to be that of Jesus. "Alfred, feed my people," said Jesus. That moment of theophany, though never repeated or paralleled in his experience, has remained the transcendental bedrock of his social-action-oriented ministry for over half a century.

As Kenneth Leech puts it, "To divide contemplation from prophecy is to damage and maybe destroy both." We must remember the prophet Micah's formulation of what God asks of us: "to do justice, and to love kindness, *and* to walk humbly with your God" (Micah 6:8, italics mine).

The forces, however, which stand in the way of activists being people of prayer are formidable. Let us take a detailed look at them.

Chapter

Guilt
and
Grace

I don't need my spirituality as one more thing that I feel guilty about not getting together!

Mary, a suburban pastor

Just below the surface of our lives most of us have a reservoir of guilt about religious matters. It does not take a lot to put us in touch with this guilt. Bring up the issue of prayer practices among serious Christians, and most of us will utter an inward cry of "guilty as charged"—even before any charges are made. We have heard the message enough times in the past that we *ought* or *should* do more in the way of devotional practice; we feel convicted no matter what. And increased discussion of spiritual practices—journal keeping, centering prayer, retreats, spiritual guidance, and such—can easily activate a lot of those old *oughts*, along with the guilt that goes with them.

A seminary teacher confirms encountering such guilt around prayer in his experience with theological students. "I'm no longer surprised," Laurence Wagley reports, "that generally students' first response to the topic of prayer is to confess how little they pray. They know they ought to. They say they have a guilty conscience from neglecting prayer."[1]

Here's how Mary, pastor of a growing suburban congregation in the West, reacted to some of my ideas for integrating spiritual practice and social action:

... spiritual practice feels like something else to add to my time schedule at this point in life. Disciplined life, at least at this stage of who I am, seems to be so out of my control in terms of church and family and relationships. I don't need my spirituality as one more thing that I feel guilty about not getting together!

At that point there was a hearty chorus of "amens" from the others in the room, endorsing her sentiments. She continued:

In this stage of life, I'm pastoring in a church where spiritual discipline is not encouraged, where I would again be a leader in promoting something. Where is there a place of rest to experience inner renewal that doesn't take the week or weekend or half-day that you're all talking about? I just don't have any more of those to give. Can you get "Spirituality Lite 101" some way?

Mary's response points to the incredible workload we have come to place on pastors and the very real problem of finding time for a new activity, especially one that adds to burdens of initiative and leadership. Spiritual life leadership was not a part of the working definition of the pastoral priorities in her parish—or in so many others, for that matter. Yet she had a sense that spiritual practice may somehow be connected to a place of rest and that such practice had personal promise for her—if only it were not a source of new guilt and further overload. When Mary asked for "Spirituality Lite 101," the group of social activists in the room burst out in approving laughter. Clearly she touched some widely shared feelings.

These concerns deserve to be taken seriously. If spiritual practice is interpreted as yet another heavy burden, then who would welcome further exploration? Laurence Wagley comments, "Much recent literature on prayer and spiritual formation has taken the 'pumping iron' approach. The central theme is 'try harder.'"[2] An article he wrote seeking to counteract this tendency is appropriately titled "Prayer for the Hurried, the Undisciplined and the Disorganized."

My conviction is that the spiritual practice appropriate for a person is not so much a discipline as a "coming home." It is the response to an invitation to let one's heart gravitate toward its true Home, its abiding center. One of the characteristics I most prize in Gerald

May's guidance in contemplative practice is his constant encouragement of gentleness toward oneself:

> In all my experience as a psychiatrist and as a human being, the deepest, most pervasive pathology I have seen is the incredible harshness we have toward ourselves.... The most religious of us are so terrified of appearing selfish that we subject ourselves to unnameable internal cruelties.... I am not encouraging you to try to maintain a steady state of self-love, but simply to bring a little kindness toward yourself from time to time. Just an instant of it, just a brief interior touch. This is what gentleness means, and it is in this good atmosphere that your basic sanity can grow.... For God's sake, do not throw upon yourself the extra burden of "having" to feel kindly toward yourself.[3]

These words of gentleness are a beautiful commentary on the well-known invitation of Jesus: "Come to me, all you that are weary and are carrying heavy burdens, I will give you rest.... For my yoke is easy, and my burden is light" (Matthew 11:28, 30).

This lightness and gentleness can be ours if our central focus is simply on our inner attitude, not on a new regimen. I am drawn particularly to contemplative prayer because it is not so much doing something as being, being who one is in the presence of God. The focus is on awareness, noticing, and intention. We are encouraged to recognize that in each moment God is providing us with all we need and is indeed already praying in us and through us. We do not have to do anything, except notice, listen, and allow. All we need to do is show up.

In this mode of receptive noticing, we may well note that, for all our limitations, we do have a significant spiritual life. When I started having sessions with a spiritual director, I began with considerable guilt about the poverty of my spiritual life. One of the first wonderful revelations was to discover how much prayer and devotion to God was already going on within me. Other colleagues have shared similar feelings.

Anne, a pastor who was part of the group to which Mary made her comment, raised a related issue triggered by my personal style:

> I resonate with Mary about the guilt thing. In fact, I have talked with George about how he's much more an introvert than I am

in the kinds of prayer he uses. It's really hard for me to follow guided meditation, for instance. I just go somewhere else in my mind. I don't need another layer of guilt about not being able to pray the way everybody else says to.

Anne raises an important issue. She is a self-avowed, practicing extrovert. She is right that I am not. Further, she contends that some of the prayer forms that I lead at meetings and retreats may be fine for me, but she experiences them as so alien that they become a source of guilt.

Anne's experience is an important reminder that we each have unique, God-given personalities and that these personalities affect the way we relate to God as well as to each other. She keeps pushing me to include more singing and music in our meetings and retreats, and I would do well to heed her suggestions. The point is that our concern for spiritual practice should always take the form of an invitation, recognizing and allowing for personal differences and providing plenty of space for a variety of forms. At the same time, we should encourage Anne, or anyone else, to explore some unfamiliar terrain which may not seem to serve her dominant personality type, but which may minister to a more submerged part of her being.

My wife has a special place on her desk for a lovely pottery jar which she received as a gift. It is labeled "Shoulds and Oughts" and has a large cork top that fits perfectly in the mouth of the jug. The way to reduce guilt around our spiritual practice is to place our "shoulds" and "oughts" in a jar as they arise—and keep the cork on. In other words, God does not want us to be dwelling on our supposed shortcomings. We are a forgiven people. So for starters let us put these in the jar:

"You *should* be more spiritual."
"You *ought* to go on retreat at least once a year."
"You *should* pray when you start your day."
"Journal-keeping is what any serious Christian *ought* to do."
"Every pastor *should* be a spiritual director."

In doing this, we take the "shoulds" off our backs and from around our necks and place them in God's hands.

Spirituality Lite 101

Be still, and know that I am God!   Psalm 46:10

Let us make a try at a curriculum for "Spirituality Lite 101," a (hopefully) nonguilt-inducing introduction to a deepening spiritual awareness. I will invite you to some surrender, some stillness, and some noticing. I will not ask you to *do* anything in the normal sense, though an attitude of active receptivity is called for. You do not have to bring your intercession list, your journal, or your tapes for meditation. Just bring your heart and your inner hunger.[4]

A CONTEMPLATIVE PRAYER EXPERIENCE

- To begin, I ask you to settle into a comfortable position. Perhaps shifting in your chair or wherever you are sitting would make you more comfortable. . . .

- Then as you take your next several breaths, invite your breath into any tightened muscles you might wish to relax, such as your shoulders, your jaw, or your neck. (Recall that one of the biblical metaphors for resistance to God is "stiff-necked!")[5] Let the breath seem to flow into these tightened muscles. Upon exhaling, you may feel the muscles begin to let go of some tension. Do this several times. . . .

- As you are able, simply surrender to the astounding reality of God's personal care for you. You are loved through and through by our loving Creator God. You are loved and embraced—your past, your present, your future. You are important and valued by God as a significant member of the human family.

- Let these words of the psalmist resonate within you:

  For it was you who formed my inward parts;
      you knit me together in my mother's womb. . . .
  Your eyes beheld my unformed substance.
  In your book were written
      all the days that were formed for me,
      when none of them as yet existed. (Psalm 139:13, 16)

- This does not mean everything in life is how you might like it. But it does mean that God walks with you through each moment, that God cares deeply, and that your life is touched by grace. In the Bible this intimacy with God is beautifully described as being connected to the one in whom "we live and move and have our being" (Acts 17:28).

- Nothing is required of you. Simply be aware of the present moment, and offer it to God. In this moment, even as you read this, you have everything you need. Just take in the fullness of the moment, without analyzing or judging it as good or bad.

- In this nonjudgmental way, let your eyes gently, lovingly, gaze upon what is around you....

- In the same nonjudgmental way, let your ears gently take in any sounds present, including often unnoticed background sounds. Just allow the sounds to be....

- Now be aware of life within yourself. Without judging, notice your mood...your concerns....

- Allow your noticing to go deeper, touching your deepest longings and yearnings. Acknowledge them lovingly. Surrender them in this moment to God. In other words, "Be still, and know that I am God" (Psalm 46:10). If you can, simply rest in this presence, with alert receptivity and surrender....

- Then, when you are ready to go on, offer whatever prayer honestly emerges from you—whether a prayer of thanksgiving, intercession, or guidance. As you move on, allow your surrender and your receptivity to flow with you. Nurture your awareness of the present moment in whatever you do.

"The sacrament of the present moment" is a phrase coined by Jean-Pierre de Caussade, an eighteenth-century Jesuit priest. It beautifully describes the sacredness and completeness of each moment in which we are fully alive. The poet E. E. Cummings describes the discovery of the richness of the present moment in this way:

> i thank You God for most this amazing
> day:for the leaping greenly spirits of trees
> and a blue true dream of sky;and for everything
> which is natural which is infinite which is yes
>
> (i who have died am alive again today,
> and this is the sun's birthday;this is the birth
> day of life and of love and wings:and of the gay
> great happening illimitably earth)
>
> how should tasting touching hearing seeing
> breathing any—lifted from the no
> of all nothing—human merely being
> doubt unimaginable You?
>
> (now the ears of my ears awake and
> now the eyes of my eyes are opened)[6]

May you partake of the sacrament of this present moment...and of the next moment...and the next....

The concluding part of this short course surfaced for me in the context of a national board meeting of the social action organization for which I work. A committee was finishing its work when I walked into the room. Jim, the committee chair, had chosen a particular passage as a devotional reading because, as he put it, "the number one issue for social justice advocates is drawing the line so as not to feel one has to do everything." Here is what Jim read from *A Testament of Devotion*, by the Quaker philosopher Thomas Kelly:

> [A concern] is a particularization of *my* responsibility...in a world too vast and a lifetime too short for me to carry all responsibilities. My cosmic love, or the Divine Lover loving within me, cannot accomplish its full intent, which is universal saviourhood, within the limits of three score years and ten. But the Loving Presence does not burden us equally with all things, but considerately puts upon each of us just a

few central tasks, as emphatic responsibilities. For each of us these special undertakings are our share in the joyous burdens of love.[7]

This reading stopped me in my tracks. This is a Word, a grace-filled Word of God, I thought, both for me and for others like me. The reading concluded with Kelly's comment regarding "all the multitude of [other] good things that need doing":

> Toward them all we feel kindly, but we are dismissed from active service in most of them. And we have an easy mind in the presence of desperately real needs which are not our direct responsibility. We cannot die on *every* cross nor are we expected to.[8]

I was awed by the amazing relevance of this short collection of articles and talks. Though Thomas Kelly died in 1941 from a heart attack at age forty-three, he left a remarkable legacy—a contemplative vision of social action! What healing words for those of us called to be agents of social healing!

Kelly's words cry out for noticing, for allowing them to lead us and to center us. Hear him further:

> Social concern is the dynamic Life of God at work in the world, made special and emphatic and unique, particularized in each individual or group who is sensitive and tender in the leading-strings of love. A concern is God-initiated, often surprising, always holy, for the Life of God is breaking through into the world. Its execution is in peace and power and astounding faith and joy, for in unhurried serenity the Eternal is at work in the midst of time, triumphantly bringing all things up unto Himself.[9]

Perhaps there is no more important Word for us activists whose lives are too busy, who hear so many urgent voices, and who care about so many ongoing tragedies. God "does not burden us equally with all things," but only with certain callings and tasks which are to be our part in the "joyous burdens of love." And mark this: "We cannot die on every cross nor are we expected to."[10] Rather, we are to focus on the particular arena to which God leads us. And there we are to labor in peace and power and faith and joy, rooted in "the unhurried serenity of the Eternal" at work. Thanks be to God!

End of class!

Chapter

3

The Silent Tyranny of the Modern Worldview

To begin our look at another obstacle to uniting prayer and social action, let me describe two recent gatherings, one of scientists and intellectuals, the other of church activists.

"The limits of scientific knowledge" was the theme of an intensive workshop which brought together twenty intellectuals for intensive dialogue.[1] A profound humility pervaded the discussions. A mathematician surmised that mathematics is so riddled with truths that appear random rather than logical that it may increasingly become a field of experimentation with less of a claim to absolute truth. A biologist illustrated the incompleteness of knowledge by describing the great difficulty biologists are having achieving a precise definition of life. Cosmologists reported the limits they confront when they ponder what, if anything, preceded the universe's birth. A psychologist commented, "We may be headed toward a situation where knowledge is too complicated to understand."[2] And a major foundation is considering a program to get educational systems to put more emphasis on what is unknown and unknowable.

At the gathering of church social activists, the topic was obstacles to prayer. Science emerged quickly as a serious stumbling block. "Our very psyches," complained an ecumenical staffer from Albany, New York, "have been formed by the scientism of the last centuries, and its rationalism has been robbing us of our ability to enter into the noncognitive realities of life."

"I've been brought up with science and its reaction to the 'superstitious' domination of culture by the church," said Robert, a pastor in a northern state. A deeply spiritual person, he testified poignantly to how deep the scientific worldview lies within us:

> I've been schooled in this through my father, as well as decades of formal schooling. In traditional science, if you can't see it, feel it, or touch it, it's not real. The only thing that's real is what can be measured. Everything else is considered superstition, just mindless and completely unimportant. And supposedly the only people that really take "the spiritual" seriously are Sunday school teachers—and they're women and pansy preachers. But "real men" measure things with rulers. So taking seriously the idea that the spiritual is the most real runs against the centuries old foundation of my education.

Sharon, a lay activist also from a northern state, spoke about how this worldview had marginalized her. "In my family of engineers and such, everyone is rule and ruler oriented; if you don't have the facts, you don't count. As someone whose life is really based—I finally realized—on feelings, I am starting to get a little bit of acknowledgment from them that maybe, just maybe, there's something valuable from the other side."

A pastor in the South, Helen, added that thinking in terms of measurements was foreign to her and that life had been difficult for her in a male-dominated church because her language and thought patterns were so different. "Even in the church," she sighed, "what I think often really doesn't count."

From entirely different points of view, each of these gatherings was critiquing the traditional scientific worldview with its belief in the unlimited power and relevancy of the scientific method of the Enlightenment. The traditional scientific worldview has taken a toll on our religious practice. Our confidence in the power of prayer and ritual to effect material change has been eroded, for prayer has mostly been relegated to an inner, "spiritual" realm. The life of the "real world" has seemed sealed off from the power of prayer and ritual. We have been left in the material realm of institutions and power structures without a voice or a vocabulary for prayer.

Unmasking the Materialistic Worldview

In this view there is no heaven, no spiritual world, no God, no soul—nothing but material existence. . . .

Walter Wink

As both of these meetings indicate, this worldview is no longer so unquestioned that it seems invisible. Its protective shield of anonymity is being stripped away, and it is being named for what it is and identified for its idolatry. This worldview has been named "materialistic," and some have traced it to Democritus (ca. 460–ca. 370 B.C.E.). The materialist perspective is ruthless toward anything transcendent, as Walter Wink writes:

> In this view, there is no heaven, no spiritual world, no God, no soul—nothing but material existence and what can be known through the five senses and reason. The spiritual world is an illusion. There is no higher self; we are mere complexities of matter, and when we die we cease to exist except as the chemicals and atoms that once constituted us. This materialistic worldview has penetrated deeply even into many Christians, causing them to ignore the spiritual dimensions of systems or the spiritual resources of faith.[3]

According to Wink, serious damage has been wrought by the materialistic worldview: "To a degree far beyond current recognition, the myth of materialism has served as such an integrating agent for modern society, but it has been an integration bought at the cost of what is most human, most aesthetic, and most meaningful in life."[4] Thus the modern worldview has emptied our perceived universe of much spiritual reality. The classical worldview of science is materialistic, and nonmaterial reality has had a difficult time justifying its place in our consciousness.

Although few religious persons have held to a doctrine of materialism, its philosophical consequences have been substantial. Indeed, there have been rebellions. The Romantic movement and the Wesleyan movement, with its religion of the heart, are notable examples. But the power of materialistic science and philosophy has deeply eroded our sense of ultimate mystery, unseen reality, God, and the meaningfulness of prayer.

In the face of this materialistic threat, Christian theology posited a supernatural realm. Most theologians, according to Wink, whether from liberal, neo-orthodox, or traditional and conservative theological circles, "conceded earthly reality to modern science and preserved a privileged 'spiritual' realm immune to confirmation or refutation."[5] Both the spiritual and earthly realms were "hermetically sealed" from each other.

This enforced separation of the material from the spiritual also served to hermetically seal off social issues and social change (part of the realm of earth) from matters of devotion and piety (part of the spiritual realm). Concern for society, including the social and natural sciences operated within this sealed materialistic universe.

It is important, however, to keep the Enlightenment in historical perspective. As Canadian theologian Gregory Baum points out, it was conceived of as a project of emancipation, and its philosophers "regarded reason as the organ of human emancipation."[6] Reason would enable people to analyze the forms of oppression and guide them in their struggle for emancipation. Not only was reason to lead to emancipation from myths, fables, and prerational ideas, it challenged inherited ideas which served to lock people into traditional hierarchies. As Baum says, "The enlightenment thinkers also understood emancipation as liberation from physical oppression....The feudal order, aristocracy and monarchy held wide sectors of the population in bondage. Freedom promised participation. Freedom meant democracy."[7] Much that we value is inherited from the Enlightenment. As Sandra Schneiders points out, the eighteenth-century Enlightenment canonized the principle that "the ultimate criterion of true human knowledge" is "free critical investigation, not the exercise of authority."[8]

The problem lies in the reductionism of the Enlightenment worldview. Emancipation, for many, necessitated liberation from any transcendent, spiritual reality. Further, the methods that were so successful in the physical sciences were felt to be applicable to all of life, to the extent that, as Baum says, "Today the scientific Enlightenment has become an obstacle to freedom." Increasingly the human goals of freedom, equality, and participation were over-shadowed by scientific, technical reason:

> The Enlightenment trusted in science, in scientific reason and tech-nological control. Eventually, it has been argued, the Enlightenment thinkers applied the scientific method to all aspects of human life; the entire world became a machine for them which could be scientifical-ly known and technologically controlled; values, vision, freedom, the quality of the human, all of these aims disappeared under the pressure of technological rationality. . . . And because human feelings did not fit into scientifically defined framework, they often burst out in new forms of irrationality.[9]

Originally the scientific worldview was an agent of freedom, an intrinsic part of the Enlightenment. But a worldview is, in New Testament terminology, a "power"; and as powers are prone to do, worldviews can become rebellious against God and seek to shut out the transcendent. They seek to become total. In this case the notion was that a single method, modeled on mathematics, could open up the possibility of unlimited knowledge in every area of inquiry. According to Schneiders, "a major breakthrough in the intellectual life of the twentieth century" has been the realization that such an approach "was wrongheaded from the start."

Embracing a New Worldview

A new conceptual worldview is already in place, latently.
Walter Wink

Actually, the movement beyond a deadening rationalism has been underway for some time. Theologians Gregory Baum and Sandra Schneiders distinguish between the Early Enlightenment, when the mathematical-scientific model was applied to all of life whether appropriate or not, and the Late Enlightenment, when this deadening rationalism was vigorously undermined. The so-called "masters of suspicion," Marx, Freud, Nietzsche, and the Frankfurt School of social thinkers, brought an "Enlightenment critique of Enlightenment," undermining the overwhelming rationalism through recovery of the emotions, unmasking false consciousness, developing sociological theory, critiquing patriarchal domination, and questioning traditional truths. According to Baum, "while the Early Enlightenment was hostile to religion, the Late Enlightenment, while often appearing unreligious, was basically open to religion."[10]

Summing up, Walter Wink contends that a "new integral world-view has only just come of age.... I conclude that a very rapid and fundamental sea change has been taking place in our worldview that has passed largely unrecognized but is everywhere felt. A new conceptual worldview is already in place, latently, and can be triggered by its mere articulation."[11]

This integral worldview is worlds apart from the mechanical, materialistic worldview, and also from a spiritual worldview in which religious and earthly aspects are sealed off from each other. The integral worldview comprehends the spiritual and the material coexisting. All reality has a spiritual aspect, an interiority, as well as an outer, physical manifestation.

I believe an appreciation of this emerging integral worldview addresses the obstacles to prayer in the modern, mechanical, rationalistic worldview identified earlier in this chapter. If spiritual reality inheres in the interiority of all reality, personal or social, human or nonhuman, then our Christian understanding is in no way sealed off from, or irrelevant to, the universe in which we live. Rather than being irrelevant to human life, our spiritual temperament, tradition, and training are special gifts and insights into the inner life of the world, both its institutions and its individuals. If we have, in the words of the author of Ephesians, "the power to comprehend, with all the saints, what is the breadth and length and height and depth, and to know the love of Christ that surpasses knowledge" (Ephesians 3:18-19), and if this applies to the very physical-spiritual world in which we live, then we have a great treasure indeed! Furthermore, if our Christian language and tradition help reveal how things are and how things ought to be in the actual world in which we live, then our practices of prayer and ritual, rather than leading us out of this world, offer us a language, a voice, and a vocabulary for addressing, in the name of God, the very interiority of the (supposedly) material realm of institutions and power structures.

I agree with Walter Bruggemann that in our era God is at work dismantling the unduly rationalistic, controlling, and dominating characteristics of the Enlightenment worldview. We live between the in-breaking of a new worldview and its full realization when it becomes the new common sense. With respect to our most basic understandings of our world, we are living between the times.

Though the old worldview is disintegrating, it still can have a hold on us, despite our knowing better. But we do have a choice whether to live our lives, preach our sermons, and do our social action in the fading consciousness of the old worldview or in the reality of the new consciousness. I believe God's invitation is to live in the integral worldview.

Chapter

Tool of
Domination
or
Wellspring
of
Resistance?

The fear is that spirituality is a tool of the Religious Right to refocus the energy which has been devoted to justice.
An ecumenical relief worker in Iowa

Since 1972 I have been in a union job, and yet in twenty years I have heard any number of anti-labor sermons, but very few that might be considered pro-labor.
A lay activist in New York

Another obstacle to integrating spiritual practice with action is the aversion many social activists have developed to religious practice because Christianity has been widely used to justify injustice. Such misuse has a long history. Christianity since Constantine has been the religion of empire, establishment, and status quo.

My impression is that we are dealing here with the most difficult obstacle to the unity of prayer and action among social activists. Overwhelmingly, what social activists see in churches is the unity of prayer and inaction in the face of injustice and evil, or worse, the overt use of prayer and spiritual practice to justify injustice and callousness toward racism, sexism, heterosexism, and classism.

Gregory Baum views this aversion to religious language with empathy:

For many Christians committed to social justice, religious language has become suspect because the meaning assigned to this language by the dominant culture legitimates the existing order despite its injustices. For this reason these Christians often refuse to speak about inwardness and religious experience. They search for a secular vocabulary. Sometimes they create the impression that they have little interest in the openness of faith to the divine voice and the divine presence.[1]

This sense of alienation from religious language and practice is constantly reinforced, and not only by fringe figures who murder abortion doctors or justify such killing or by traditions that deny women ordination. Such alienation stems as well from experience within mainline Protestant traditions that on a denominational level generally articulate justice perspectives. Clergy are led to know that being a social activist will not help them advance in their career. Pastors wishing to be agents of social transformation in the community are forced in most cases to perform an intricate balancing act between their personal social vision and their congregation's overriding concern for institutional maintenance. Though trained with the expectation of becoming pastor-theologian-spiritual guide to laypeople working for social justice in the world, a pastor typically must settle for encouraging an incremental increase in social tolerance among congregants. God willing, she or he may be able to work with a small group in the congregation or community to address injustice from a faith perspective, hoping all the while not to alienate the pillars of the congregation. The biblical definition of the people of God as a light to the nations, a beacon of hope, bears little relationship in most white churches to the reality of a congregation of conservative to moderate, status quo-oriented people.

The Hegemony of Capitalism

We might as well replace the cross with a giant brass dollar sign on the altar.
A Midwestern pastor

At the roots of this alienation is the capitulation of most religion to the powers-that-be. "Most religious organizations," according to Harry Magdoff and Paul Sweezy, "have served as major defenders and rationalizers of the existing order. And the ruling classes in turn support and rely on the dominant religions in their countries to blind the exploited masses to the causes of their misery and to keep resistance in check."[2]

The powers-that-be which religion serves are a subtle combination of oppressive systems. Some of these interlocking powers are under sharp attack, such as racism, sexism, and increasingly, heterosexism. But there is another power more rarely named against which criticism today is quite muted—capitalism. The general silence regarding capitalism makes it all the more insidious.

What Paul Tillich wrote in Germany in 1930 is still true today:

> Almost without exception, behind Western democracy stand the great capitalists as the group that upholds the structure of the state: not unequivocally, frequently divided among themselves, often restricted by powers that are not yet absorbed by the market, but always present, and finally always victorious.... What is to be condemned is that they operate unseen, irresponsibly and indirectly. Concealed by democracy, they utilize it and undermine it, they bear it and at the same time destroy it.[3]

The philosopher-activist Antonio Gramsci was the first to describe capitalism as having "hegemony," a preponderant influence, over all the manifestations of human culture. Confined for years to an Italian prison cell, Gramsci came to see how the agents of wealth exercise their hegemony through a combination of force and consent. This hegemony, stated Gramsci, is "protected by the armour of coercion."[4] Brute force stands as the final enforcer. But since the use of naked force in a democratic society can be counterproductive, the force is made to "appear to be based on the consent of the majority, expressed by the so-called organs of public opinion"—news media, associations, lobbyists, educational institutions, the book industry, and cultural institutions.[5] Fraud and corruption, Gramsci said, are held in reserve for use when the maintenance of hegemony becomes problematic and the use of force is too risky. The wielders of power must, of course, take some account of the interests of the groups over which hegemony is to be exercised. Thus compromises must be made (such as capital makes with labor), but the compromises must not endanger the essential, that is, the maintenance of ultimate economic power.

The powers-that-be require that religion too serve the legitimation of the status quo, especially in the economic realm. The critical role of religion as an arbiter of values must be co-opted. A certain flexibility can be allowed and, in fact, is necessary. Occasional religious voices can be allowed to criticize the most glaring injustices of the economic system, but various means will be used to assure that religious bodies in the main provide support for the capitalist system. Among these means are the power to deny the tax-deductibility of contributions. As Gramsci points out, the state will use whatever means necessary to assure the capitalist system's ultimate hegemony over organized religion. The history of the Federal Bureau of Investigation's surveillance of progressive religious movements and leaders such as Martin Luther King, Jr., Georgia Harkness, and Harry F. Ward illustrates the lengths to which government will go to control dissent.[6]

Such heavy-handed means of control, however, are not generally desirable to the powers-that-be. Much more desirable is the creation of such an overpowering general climate of legitimation for capitalism (called "free enterprise," "market economy," "American way of life," and so forth) that religion becomes self-regulating. Hence, any form of theology based upon empowerment of the marginalized, such as liberation theology and women's theology, will before long suffer vigorous attack from within the churches or from generously funded nonprofit parachurch organizations.

On the congregational level, the churches' ethos is thoroughly imbued with capitalist values. Here is how one pastor described a particularly blatant form of capitalist hegemony in a church she was serving:

I've just begun serving a rural church here in the Midwest. Once again I am facing the survival mentality and the idolatry of money.... The more I learn, the more I see that there is a dollar sign hovering near almost everything this sickly church does, considers, or even *is*. This spiritual idolatry is reflected in the attitudes of the leaders, the worship service, the policies for the building's use, the agenda of meetings, and so much more. We might as well replace the cross with a giant brass dollar sign on the altar. Perhaps prayer and preaching are the only things that can wrest this idol from its throne. I will have calluses on my knees before it happens, I'm sure!

Should a pastor even begin to proclaim a serious indictment of capitalism, let alone act upon it, his or her tenure would likely be in serious doubt. The case of St. Mark's United Methodist Church, Camache, Iowa, is instructive. In this one remarkable instance, a congregation with an outspoken solidarity with liberation struggles and an informed critique of capitalism endured for thirteen years before ecclesiastical authorities and disaffected members were able to end the experiment. A core of the faithful continue, but as a small, independent, lay-led Christian base community.[7]

Tragically, many churches embrace Mammon and the capitalistic ethos with a mind-boggling enthusiasm. Just a block from four of the world's largest hotel-casinos in Las Vegas is the Shrine of the Most Holy Redeemer, a Roman Catholic church where worshipers are invited to place casino chips in the offering plate. These chips can also be used to make purchases at the church gift shop. There, in exchange for a five-dollar donation to the church building fund, you receive a souvenir gaming chip with a likeness of Jesus Christ on it.

The Capitalist Threat to Spiritual Life

"Eternity is found in Calvin Klein bottles."
John Kavanaugh

Given the hegemony of the capitalist ethos over American religion, it would be impossible for the spiritual lives of American Christians not to be affected. Maintaining the inner allegiance of the individual is of critical importance to the powers-that-be.

A critical feature of capitalism is the drive to maximize personal and corporate profit. The operation of the system depends upon institutionalization of greed. A leading management consultant paid tribute to this principle when he protested a particular health insurance proposal "for being antithetical to the American ethic" because it would "penalize profitability."[8]

Another feature of capitalism is the powerful pressure to transform every possible aspect of life into a commodity, something

TOOL OF DOMINATION OR WELLSPRING OF RESISTANCE? *43*

objectified, which can be bought or sold. In the process the item is transformed from something that arises within a matrix of human relations into an object torn from these relationships. A simple example is the transformation of orange juice from a food grown for sustenance to a crop harvested to make money, and then to a listing on a commodity futures market, where it becomes a tool of speculators seeking a quick profit.

In a commodity-oriented economy things and persons are objectified; they became the objects of vast schemes of manipulation. Enormous forces are at work to create "needs" in us, to persuade us to buy one thing or the other. We are objects of endless marketing campaigns, often of remarkable creativity and sophistication. Even if we never looked at television—which devotes an ever-increasing amount of air time to commercials—we could not avoid billboards, bus and subway ads, telemarketing intrusions into our dinner hour, inundations of junk mail advertising, or massive amounts of newspaper and periodical advertising. The manipulators of the market never cease in their search for new ways to get their message across. Advertisers are exceedingly inventive in finding new ways to place commercial messages in places where we cannot avoid them, such as on computer screens, in the naming of sporting events and sports arenas, and on the clothing of celebrities.

Roman Catholic ethicist John Kavanaugh points out that this commodity-dominated economy has created a "culture of lost interiority." The intrinsic value of things is radically devalued. And the intrinsic value of human beings is a casualty as well. What matters is the surface appearance. To an enormous extent in our consumer culture, we trade in surface images. As Kavanaugh says, "We look at images of images and fancy them real."[9]

Seeing ourselves as entities whose value is instrumental rather than intrinsic, we absorb the culture gospel of the capitalist consumer society which proclaims that our worth lies in what we are able to produce. Our value must be demonstrated in something tangible, with a payoff, with marketability.

This consumer-ism—the reduction of everything to commodities for consumption—creates a culture with debilitating characteristics and serious consequences for religious thought and practice. This consumerism is in fact an alternative religion, an idolatry. Kavanaugh declares:

> Buying and consuming have become vehicles for experiencing the sacred. The infinite longing of the human heart has been introjected into products—the newest, the best, the costliest, the always interminably improved. Our malls are "cathedrals of consumption." Eternity is found in Calvin Klein bottles. Infiniti in a Japanese automobile. One's heart, no longer a throne wherein the transcendent personal God might dwell, no longer engaged by a knowing and loving trinitarian encounter of other persons, is restless until it rests— now anchored or even chained by the promise of possessions. Thus, accumulation is king.[10]

The capitalist consumer ideology is all-pervasive, affecting the way we think, feel, and relate to other people. It deadens us to relationship, to human values, and to caring while bedeviling us with endless possibilities for accumulating possessions. It promotes unrelieved competition in every area of life. Its seduction provides an enormous counterforce to our efforts to create communities of compassion and justice. Attempts to introduce just institutions, such as a comprehensive, egalitarian national health care system, frequently fall victim to the rationale of the almighty marketplace.

Intimacy, too, is a casualty, for intimacy depends upon valuing what is intrinsic. Caring that is based upon what another can do for me is not genuine caring. It reduces the other to a commodity. True caring cherishes the other for who that person is intrinsically, not for what I can gain.

The key point here is that this loss of interiority and intimacy threatens the very foundation of prayer. Prayer involves an intimate relation to the Divine Mystery—valued, appreciated, and loved for who God is, not for what the payoff will be. Time spent in prayer, meditation, and contemplation does not necessarily have an immediate or obvious payoff. It may, in fact, undermine our passion to climb the career ladder or increase our sense of burden for others rather than dull it. As a Long Island pastor observed:

> The whole underlying assumption of capitalism is that by my effort I can achieve my goal—if I work hard enough and have

the right connections. Prayer, on the other hand, says your effort is worth nothing. It's all given. You need to let go of your effort. Prayer is relationship, something we're not too good at in our culture unless we're using the relationship for some end. Prayer is simply for its own sake.

Genuine Prayer as Subversion

To clasp the hands in prayer is the beginning of an uprising against the disorder of the world.

Karl Barth

Although the powers-that-be will attempt to use any form of religion and religious devotion to justify themselves, prayer of complete surrender to God and prayer for the Reign of God do not make sense to a consumerist culture. Ultimately genuine prayer is subversive. As Kavanaugh notes, praying is cultural resistance. Prayer is a kind of guerrilla warfare against the powers of domination, against the hegemony of the capitalist system. "The pursuit of prayerful life," says Kenneth Leech, "sets us in isolation and opposition to the mainstream, mammon-directed culture in which we live."

Prayer leads us away from acquisitiveness and toward sharing. It directs us from surface goods such as reputation, status, and personal power toward inner goods—faith, hope, and love. It opens our grasping hand and encourages our surrender. It moves us from competition with our neighbor toward compassion for our neighbor, and it opens the doors of intimacy with self, neighbor, and the Holy One.

Thus, genuine prayer engages in tearing the mask off of the systematic oppression of the powers-that-be who consider themselves our rightful earthly lords, revealing how these systems of domination have distorted religious life to their own ends. True appropriation of Christian faith and practice is a subversive act that undermines the systems of domination in our own internal life, and in church and community life. As Karl Barth declares, "To clasp the hands in prayer is the beginning of an uprising against the disorder of the world."

If we refrain from using the language of the Spirit, if we avoid prayer or spiritual practice because they have been debased and distorted, we grant the purveyors of consumer culture a monopoly on religious language. We are then bereft of historically tested forms of communication with the Holy, and people are left to believe that Christianity is properly the religion of the oppressive systems.

On one level we should accept the fact that capitalist hegemony bends most religion to its purposes. As long as capitalism reigns, it will seek to do this and will accomplish it. This is what it means to live in a capitalist system. Its infection is systemic.

But on another level, we should never acquiesce or be comfortable with this hegemony. We should nurture a deep sense of dis-ease about this state of affairs. Equipped with an understanding of the ideologically totalitarian systems of oppression, we are better able to reclaim elements of Christian life for the prophetic message. Was this not the model of the Hebrew prophets? Was not this the way of Jesus and the earliest church? As women's advocates are properly urging women "to take back the night," progressive Christians should be taking back spirituality and prayer from the clutches of oppression-serving religion. We must assure that the realm of spiritual practice is not the monopoly of the powers-that-be.

The Psalms can be a very helpful starting point for recovering prayer as the voice of authentic protest. In a forthcoming chapter I shall discuss how many laments in the Psalms originated in the struggle against oppression of the marginalized within ancient Israel.

Another important resource for us is the Lord's Prayer. In a fascinating examination of this prayer, Michael Crosby points out that in the early church "the discipline of the secret" (*disciplina arcana*) required that the Lord's Prayer be kept secret from those not baptized, not only for pedagogical reasons but for reasons of security: "It represented a viewpoint and ideology counter to that which legitimated the institutions of that day."[11] Crosby continues:

> Most, if not all, of the phrases of the Our Father called for the creation of conditions on earth that would be considered counter to those of first- and second-century environments.
>
> Looking at those times and reflecting on the presence of Jesus in history, I can only conclude that the Our Father was a subversive

prayer. Even though it was a declaration that summarized praise and petition, for those without faith it summarized a threat and delegitimation.[12]

In reclaiming the Lord's Prayer, the laments and protests of the Psalms, and the language and practice of prayer, we as modern subversives are reappropriating our rightful heritage.

Chapter

The Crisis
in Biblical
Authority

Liberals and radicals have given up on the Bible as a spiritual paradigm, as a guide for spiritual discovery and action.
Robert, northern pastor

Another obstacle to unity between spiritual practice and social action has to do with our unresolved ambivalence about the basic touchstone of our Christian faith, the Bible. As I was leading a retreat with a Christian social action group from upstate New York, I was struck by the deep undertone of hostility toward the Bible. Concluding that it would be best for these resentments to be out in the open, I proposed that we borrow a practice from gestalt psychotherapy and give everyone a chance to talk *to* the Bible. Getting the group's assent, I placed a Bible on a low table in the middle of our circle and invited each person to address it honestly and directly with their negative feelings. Here are excerpts from what we said:

SHARON: Bible, I accuse you of being duplicitous. You support this side and then that side. You let people feel superior, even when you also say we're not supposed to do that. You let people feel haughty and condemn others using your scriptures to justify themselves. And besides, you're so complicated that I have a hard time staying with you. I think I ought to, but then I can't stand it; I back off. That's why I'm taking this Disciple Bible study course—to force myself to live with the enemy. So far

I'm not liking it. I like talking with people, but I don't like reading you.

VICKI: There are things in you that I'd like children to internalize, but I don't think they can because you have turned them off to the truth. Unless they are very careful, they're going to run into the other clutter while trying to get the good stuff. If only we could have a shorter version of you that left out all the slaughtering—the annihilation of every man, woman, and child, ass and ox and everything else—because somebody gets God angry.

GEORGE: You can't keep straight what's myth, what's history, or what's fact. It's like you don't even care about keeping those things straight! Take your Gospel of John, with these long orations by Jesus. You know that these aren't Jesus' own historical words. You mislead a lot of people; they don't ever think about who wrote what, when, or why. You're treated like an icon, instead of an incredible, complex collection of books gathered over much time and from many sources.

SHARON: Bible, I can't stand the way you've allowed yourself to be abused and misrepresented. This passivity is so foolish. You're just standing there, letting people use you against one another. It's ridiculous. I know you're God's message. But you're so frustrating! Your language is so clumsy and awkward. Not only that, but over the years you've had interpreters who've added on layers of personal issues and vendettas.

STAN: I really have trouble with parts of you—on the women's issue, the gay issue, slavery, and particularly the violence. If I were going to buy a book, I would not buy you. I think that you've caused a plague, a terrible battle over whose Bible you are, because you fight within yourself.

These comments reflect a crisis regarding the authority of the Bible which many social activists are experiencing. This wandering in the desert with respect to the Bible has a secularizing effect upon our social action and a corroding effect upon our practice of prayer and discernment.

Take Carl, an activist pastor. He grew up in churches that used the Bible in narrow, pietistic ways. Now as a pastor he sees the damage such a use of the Bible has wrought. He says that his "deep desire is to open up and let the Bible speak to me, to touch the core of my being"; but he finds himself focused on avoiding sounding too pious and biblical, instead of trying to liberate the Bible for himself and others. He feels trapped by these conflicting urges.

Stan, who describes himself as a "recovering Vietnam veteran," has the most trouble with the violence in scripture that is seemingly sanctioned by God. The recurring motifs of wholesale slaughter in the Hebrew scriptures are particularly disturbing to him as he works to put Vietnam behind him. "There's a lot of stuff in the Old Testament that makes me angry. I have reservations myself about spirituality, having been raised a fundamentalist. I want to be spiritual, but I don't want to be pulled back."

The wounds people carry from fundamentalist biblical interpretation can be deep. Take the case of a woman pastor in a New England village. Upset at having a woman pastor, key members of her church defiantly invited a fundamentalist clergyman to conduct regular Bible study in their homes. Then the group demanded that they be allowed to conduct the Bible study—with outside fundamentalist leadership—in the church building. According to the Bible, they contended, she, a woman, could not lead them.

Many women have deep reservations about scripture stemming from its thoroughgoing patriarchal context. How can scripture be liberating to them, they ask, when the role of women appears so marginal and God is portrayed in such a patriarchal way? Our great spiritual ancestors are supposed to be Abraham, Isaac and Jacob. What happened to the memory of Sarah, Hagar, Rebekah, Rachel, and Leah?

Christians in the gay and lesbian community and their allies must face the fact that virtually all scholars agree that, for whatever reason, all references to same-sex erotic expression in scripture are negative ones. Is this a liberating Word? they ask. In the history of the church, the Bible has been the charter for their persecution. For such persons, Bible study may indeed feel like "living with the enemy." One creative person felt called to prepare and circulate a "Biblical Self-Defense Kit" for gays and lesbians.

Another obstacle to activists being people of the Bible lies in the feeling that, while there are riches to be mined from the Bible, the mining of them is such a technical and exacting process. "You're so complicated that I have a hard time bothering to stay with you," said Sharon to the Bible. "You fight within yourself," cried Stan. Most Christians, not only lay but also clergy, lack the time and expertise to engage in serious biblical study. With the proliferation of forms of biblical criticism—literary analysis, narrative criticism, canonical criticism, feminist criticism, form criticism, and so forth—the task of unearthing an authentic reading of a text appears more daunting and forbidding than ever.

Toward a Liberating Appropriation of Scripture

Once the group on retreat seemed to have exhausted its negative feelings toward the Bible, I gave participants the opportunity to *be* the Bible and answer back to the negative things which had been said.

VICKI: As the Bible, I don't necessarily approve of everything that's in me. People should realize that I was written from the point of view of the Israelites; they should wonder what would have been written from the point of view of the Canaanites.

DOUG: My name is plural. I am books, not book. I am development and process, reporting many voices, many points of view. I express evolving understandings. So please don't judge me just by the people and the parts of my story which are unseemly. They simply reflect humanity. Judge me by where I point and where I'm going. My pages reflect the unfolding dialogue between God and humanity. Interpret me through the highest rather than the lowest. Read me through the eyes and spirit of Jesus as best you can discern. Try to feel the context and purpose of my writings.

GEORGE: It's not fair to blame me, the Bible, for everything that people do with me. A lot of people don't have a clue about the contexts in which I was written, or for what purposes. I don't know how to get through to some folks that I'm really a charter of liberation. I need your help getting that across because there are a lot of vested interests out there. These vested interests manipulate me and interpret me in ways so that much of my core message is missed. I desperately need your help. I'm limited. It may be at some point that they'll add a book or two to me, but it's not likely in the near future. I've done my thing, and I'm in your hands now.

Participants expressed genuine appreciation for the exercise. It helped me too. It seemed to enable us to clear the air somewhat of our negativity and get us more in touch with our deep positive feelings for the Bible.

I believe New Testament interpreter Sandra Schneiders would have been an enthusiastic participant in our exercise talking to and for the Bible. She has described her experience as a student of scripture as her own feminist consciousness came to full bloom, "The biblical text, for which I still had a deep love, was revealing itself to me as not only an androcentric and patriarchal document but one that had played and continues to play a major role in causing and legitimating the oppression of women in families, churches, and societies."[1] While scripture is for her "a privileged locus of the transforming encounter between God and the believer," she does not flinch from the difficulties presented by (1) the challenges of biblical criticism, (2) the use of scripture by the church to legitimize injustice, or (3) biblical texts which reflect patriarchal and oppressive milieu.

I have found Schneiders' work very helpful in confronting what she calls the current "malaise" in biblical studies. She contends, first of all, that no one approach to scripture should command a monopoly. Religious contemplation, literary analysis, psychological and sociological insights, and feminist and liberationist insights and interpretations all can be relevant alongside the historical analysis which has dominated biblical studies. The application of the rationalist, scientific method to the study of scripture has borne great fruit and will continue to do so, she insists, but it dare not be "the sole guarantee of knowledge." All methods of biblical study, she says, whether done by professionals or laypeople, need to feed the thirst which believers have for deepening the role of scripture in their lives.

Another central point stressed by Sandra Schneiders is the importance of understanding the presuppositions and self-interests involved in biblical study. This is called ideology criticism, or the unmasking of ideological distortion, and has two important aspects.

One is the *social location* of the reader, the complex web of circumstances, cares, and personal investments of the reader's life. As Schneiders says, "our presuppositions are rarely neutral or even innocent."[2] These circumstances, perspectives, and self-interests affect how we read biblical texts.

Differences in economic class, for instance, have contributed to widely differing appropriation of biblical texts. In the fourteenth century, theologians saw in scripture biblical justification for the hierarchical feudal order, with God and king at the top, gentlemen and villeins (free peasants) in the middle, and ordinary peasants and serfs at the bottom. But a common peasants' song, inspired by the biblical creation story, saw it differently and asked, mockingly:

> When Adam delved and Eve span
> Who was then the gentleman?

It was on the basis of such biblical understanding of the original equality of all before God that revolutionary preacher John Ball declared in 1381:

> My good people, things cannot go well in England, nor ever shall, till everything be made common, and there are neither villeins nor gentlemen, . . . and the lords shall be no greater masters than ourselves. . . .
>
> What have we deserved that we should be kept enslaved? We are all descended from one father and mother, Adam and Eve. . . . They have handsome houses and manors, and we the pain and travail, the rain and wind, in the fields.[3]

From American church history we know that slaves and masters saw very different messages in scripture. For slaves, the Bible was the charter of their dignity ("If anyone is in Christ, there is neither slave nor free" Galatians 3:28), but masters and their segregationist descendants justified the inferior status of African Americans by tracing their genealogy to Ham, the outcast son of Noah. While most North Americans have spiritualized the revolutionary words of Mary about bringing down the powerful from their thrones and lifting up the lowly (Luke 1:52), Nicaraguan peasants have seen in Mary a revolutionary figure, and Benedictine sisters in Mexico revere her as a prototype and agent of economic as well as spiritual liberation.

The other aspect of ideology criticism focuses on the social location of the biblical writers. There is no such thing as a fully objective interpretation, Schneiders contends. Most of the world's great texts, including those of the Bible, have been written by those she calls "the historical winners." Therefore "a hermeneutics of suspicion that unmasks ideological distortion is an indispensable component of every effort to understand" these texts.[4] Examining these texts closely, one can often discern in the text itself a struggle between contending views, often based on economic interest and the degree of social privilege or oppression.

To the South African biblical interpreter Itumeleng Mosala, the book of Micah in its final form is a "ruling class document."[5] Subsequent editings of the Micah material, he contends, downplayed the struggle waged by the oppressed class of Israel under the monarchy and stressed instead such broad issues as Yahweh's universal reign of peace (Micah 4:1) and the promise of return from exile (4:6). Mosala declares up front that his perspective is that of the black struggle against oppression in South Africa. From that perspective he sees in the text of Micah an evasion of the concrete struggle between oppressed and oppressor which he has witnessed time and again in the life of the church in South Africa.

Such an approach to scripture raises some illuminating questions. For instance, is not the social justice context of the Psalms sometimes obscured by the ideological interest of the editor(s) to extol the monarchy created by King David, a monarchy which impoverished the masses? Is the prohibition of a man lying with another man in Leviticus 18:22 based upon an alleged "scientific" understanding of that day, namely, that the male seed was quite limited and needed to be preserved for heterosexual relations in order to propagate the people? If so, then what implications are there for our contemporary interpretation and application of such passages?

It is critical for us at all points in our interpretation process to be aware of *social location*, including our own, those of interpreters we rely upon, and those of the authors of texts. This awareness is crucial in dealing with oppressive viewpoints enshrined in scripture. We need always to ask whose interests are being served by the text and in whose interest we are interpreting the text.

In the view of ideology criticism, there is an ideological struggle within scripture, based on the social location of the various writers and editors of biblical material. I find this a clarifying perspective for the ongoing battles we fight in the church today. It means that both conservatives and progressives can justify their perspective within scripture, both the advocates of a hierarchical status quo and the advocates of justice for the oppressed. Both can claim that their viewpoint is biblical. Thus, the issue between us is not whether we are biblical or not, but how in our reading of scripture we evaluate which side, finally, God is on.

The other insight I cherish from Sandra Schneiders is that there is a surplus of meaning in scripture, that there can be more there than meets the eye. A standard interpretation of the past can be superseded. New meanings can be teased out of old texts. We are not simply stuck with patriarchal, racist, homophobic, or classist renderings. The church has found ways to relativize and move beyond the prohibition of women speaking in church; it can also move beyond the Levitical or Pauline injunctions against same-sex relations.

There is a trajectory to scripture which points beyond narrow interpretations to a broader understanding of the love of God. As Doug said, speaking for the Bible, "Judge me by where I point and where I'm going." Understood within its original context, scripture frequently brakes new ground in the pursuit of justice. As Norman Gottwald says, "Surprisingly, the voice of the poor and needy sounds throughout the Bible more persistently than in any other classical literature."[6] What if controversial questions of interpretation—such as women's role, welfare, taxation, homosexuality, affirmative action, and immigration—were seen in the light of great themes of God's loving dealings with humanity and of corresponding injunctions such as the following?

> Those who say, "I love God," and hate their sisters or brothers, are liars; for those who do not love a brother or sister whom they have seen, cannot love God whom they have not seen. The commandment we have from God is this: those who love God must love their brothers and sisters also. (1 John 4:20-21)

While much damage has indeed been done using the language of the Bible, it scarcely could be otherwise, given the hegemony of the powers-that-be. There never was a time when oppressor and oppressed did not vie for their biblical interpretation and application, nor will there be such a time in the future. What more significant language would there be for oppressive systems to co-opt than that of "gospel truth"—given the role of Christianity and its scriptures in American life? There will always be an abundance of pandering to the system and its enticements.

Just as there is a kind of class struggle within scripture, there is also a kind of class struggle in the church and in its use of scripture. What we are called to do is to engage in the struggle, to bring the best of our mind, will, and strength to the struggle and finally to leave the rest to God. The battle over whether the Bible supported or decried human slavery was waged for centuries before it was resolved. The liberating message has prevailed. The liberating message undergirded abolitionists and slaves and antisegregationists, whose work has changed society and church; that change in turn enabled the securing of the liberating message in the church.

A similar struggle for interpretation rages today regarding class, gender, sexual identity, and the care of the whole creation. The struggle over interpretation is a given; the question is whether we shall enter it or, by ignoring it, allow by default the extended perpetuation of lies in the name of God.

If we do not engage in the struggle, our prayer will be feeble, lethargic, and passionless. But if we are engaged in the struggle, committed to be biblical people, and energized by the struggle we share with God, the power and strength of the biblical language of prayer, lament, celebration, and denunciation can become ours. We are a part of the liberating of scripture, both as interpreters of scripture and its trajectory, and also as "scriptors" of our lives. Let us be sure that the lives we script and the biblical interpretations we claim perform the same liberating function in our times as the Bible did in its era.

Over and over again the biblical faith bursts the shackles that the hegemonic powers would keep around it, raises troubling questions, and champions the marginalized. Repeatedly the words of scripture leap off the forgotten page and cry out against concrete circumstances of oppression, "Let my people go."

So let us, in the words of a Lutheran prayer, have "enthusiasm for the Word." Let us be agents of the Word, those through whom the Word takes flesh in our time. The language of the Psalms can serve as a starting point. They represent a hidden treasure of profound and liberating prayer which has been mostly ignored.

Chapter

Recovering the Psalms as the Voice of Protest

The Psalms, the prayer book of the Bible and the prayer book of Jesus, have been almost exclusively interpreted in individualistic ways by both conservatives and liberals. In and of itself, there is nothing wrong with this. Each of us has been strengthened in our relationship with God by reciting the familiar "God is my shepherd.... Even though I walk through the valley of the shadow of death" (Psalm 23:1, 4), or "My times are in your hands" (Psalm 31:15).

The problem is not with praying, for example, the Twenty-third Psalm in a time of personal loss or distress. The issue is the unwitting limitation of its use to that sort of nonpolitical setting. Let it remain a profound solace to us in times of personal need. But let it also be the faith statement of the migrant labor community, which walks "in the valley of the shadow of death" when forced to pick grapes in pesticide-infested fields or when challenging growers with a union organizing drive. Let it be their passionate cry when experiencing God's caring providence while gathering at table in the presence of "enemies" who would extract every possible portion of their labor product with scant regard for their health care, shelter, sanitation, or children's education.

The social context of the Psalms is widely neglected. For instance, a footnote in the NRSV New Oxford Annotated Bible calls Psalm 43 a prayer for the healing of disease, even though the psalmist specifically calls for deliverance "from those who are deceitful and unjust" and "the oppression of the enemy" (verses 1, 2).[1]

A knowledge of the historical origins of the Israelites in relation to the book of Psalms strongly undergirds a *social* perspective on the Psalms and demonstrates the special appropriateness of the language of the Psalms for protest against injustice. Biblical Israel was formed through what Norman Gottwald calls "a socio-religious revolution of confederated Yahweh-worshiping tribes in Canaan."[2] The process was not a conquest by outsiders; rather, exploited Canaanite highland peoples, joining with exodus Israelites possessing a vivid memory of deliverance from slavery in Egypt by a militant Yahweh God, overthrew the Canaanite overlords. Through this process emerged a remarkably communitarian inter-tribal social structure unique in the ancient Near East—under the worship of this Yahweh God. In this society, women and the marginalized gained a dignity unknown in Canaanite class society, and ideals of communalism emerged that are expressed in the jubilee legislation.[3]

Subsequently there occurred what Gottwald calls a "counter-revolution" through which Israel became an intensely hierarchical, stratified, centralized monarchy "like the other nations." In that era, common people in Israel became progressively poorer and increasingly alienated from their leaders.

But as in other times and places, it was the "winners," those in control, who wrote the history and shaped the traditions. Thus, the monarchy under David was extolled as the fulfillment of God's will, the model for good rulership, and the form of messianic expectation; and nowhere is this more discernible than in the Psalms.

Though the Psalms received their final form under the aegis of the temple priests during the period of the second temple in the fifth to fourth century B.C.E., they are based upon material which is older—in some cases, much older. While it is impossible to date them exactly, clues within the Psalms indicate that the origins of many of them lay in heartfelt cries to God during the time of the counterrevolution, when the common people were experiencing increasing poverty, pauperization, and marginalization. Thus, the voice of the "losers" can also be heard in Scripture.

The Psalms arose then at a time when the communitarian social structure was being replaced by a hierarchical one. Family land was being taken to form large estates. Increasing taxes were being laid upon people to fund the trappings of a centralized state. Common people were being strapped with burdensome taxes to support construction of palaces, the temple, and fortresses—and to pay for increasing armaments and a growing bureaucracy which did not have their interests at heart.

Gottwald persuasively contends that the laments in the Psalms constitute "a large-scale psalmic protest against the evils of the political economy." These laments echo a world of oppression:

> The accused and beleaguered sufferer has been charged with crimes and cruelly slandered in order to deprive him of rights, means of subsistence, good standing in the community, and even of health and freedom of movement.... "Rich" and "wicked" are often spoken of in the same breath. The oppressors spill innocent blood in their greed for gain, seize the poor in village ambushes, speak deceitfully and bring false testimony, bribe judges shamelessly, all the while trusting and boasting in their wealth and virtue while they scorn and mock the sufferer. Oppression and fraud dominate the marketplace, the innocent are brought to trial with evil schemes, creditors seize property. When this wealth of language about socioeconomic conflict is compared with and illuminated by speeches of the prophets and proverbs of the wise, there can be little doubt that an enormous part of the suffering which psalmists protest is the *pauperization of the populace* through the manipulation of debt and confiscation procedures in such a way that even the traditional courts of Israel could be used to amass wealth in defiance of the explicit laws of the community.[4]

The Israelites' past experience of a communitarian society provided an historical memory of a society seeking to be radically faithful to Yahweh, the deliverer of the oppressed. And so they cried out, through their psalmists, for Yahweh to be in their time the Deliverer that Yahweh had been to their ancestors in Egypt. There is a close kinship between the laments of the Psalms and the moral denunciations of the eighth century prophets, Amos and Micah.

I would suggest that today we Christian social activists find ourselves in a situation with many similarities to the time in which the laments and thanksgiving songs of the Psalms arose. Consider the following parallels:

- Just as the psalmists were nurtured by the collective memory of God's deliverance, so have we been nurtured by a rich memory of God's deliverance from slavery, sin, and death.

- As the psalmists were shaped by the historic achievement of a remarkably communitarian Israelite social order, so we have been nurtured, not only by that noble experiment and by Jesus' "discipleship of equals," but also by a rich heritage of movements for justice and community, such as utopian socialist communities, the labor movement, the African American civil rights movement, Christian base communities in Latin America, and church renewal movements in the United States.

- Many in the psalmists' society experienced increasing pauperization and marginalization, and we too confront a political-economic system which, while proclaiming an egalitarian ideal, continually widens the gap between the rich and the poor and middle classes. Wealth is being extracted from across the globe to benefit an ever shrinking number of transnational corporations which maintain an ever growing power over the cultures and economies of the world.

- As the psalmists felt betrayed when the religious leaders of their era became the theologians of the new hierarchical order, legitimizing the monarchy with the Yahweh-worshiping traditions, we too feel betrayed by so many prominent Christian voices who shout "Lord, Lord" and kneel in prayer as they justify economic and political exploitation and pursue a practical atheism of hard-heartedness toward the poor and outcast.

- And as the introspective psalmist knew his or her own admixture of motives ("my iniquities have overtaken me, until I cannot see" Psalm 40:12), we too know that we participate in the very evils which we abhor.

So let us boldly pray the Psalms as our prayers for social justice. As you do, I invite you to change the pronouns from "I" to "we" and "my" to "our." The Psalms were written to express the cries of a people, not just isolated individuals. And as Gottwald says, even if the psalmist is expressing the lament of an individual, it is out of the experience of a broken and ruptured social order that wracks the whole community.

As those in deep agony at the prevalence of injustice, we too may pray:

> BE GRACIOUS TO US, O GOD, FOR WE ARE IN DISTRESS;
> OUR EYES WASTE AWAY FROM GRIEF,
> OUR SOULS AND BODIES ALSO.
> FOR OUR LIVES ARE SPENT WITH SORROW,
> AND OUR YEARS WITH SIGHING
> OUR STRENGTH FAILS BECAUSE OF OUR MISERY,
> AND OUR BONES WASTE AWAY. (PSALM 31:9-10)

As ones also needing wisdom from God in the struggle against the "deceitful and unjust," we too may pray:

> O SEND OUT YOUR LIGHT AND TRUTH; LET THEM LEAD US.
> (PSALM 43:3)

As ones frustrated by God's seeming silence and acquiescence with evil, we too may pray:

> YOU HAVE SEEN, O GOD; DO NOT BE SILENT!...
> WAKE UP! BESTIR YOURSELF FOR OUR DEFENSE...
> (PSALM 35:22A, 23A).

Also, empowered by God to claim our voices, to name and expose those doing evil and to declare their evil as godless, we may declare:

> THEIR EYES STEALTHILY WATCH FOR THE HELPLESS;
> THEY LURK IN SECRET LIKE A LION IN ITS COVERT;
> THEY LURK THAT THEY MAY SEIZE THE POOR;
> THEY SEIZE THE POOR AND DRAG THEM OFF IN THEIR NET.
> (PSALM 10:8B-9)

And as ones who trust the hand of the delivering God to lead us through rough and rocky terrain, we can offer our praise:

> Our steps are made firm by God,
>> when God delights in our way;
> though we stumble, we shall not fall headlong,
>> for God holds us by the hand. (Psalm 37:23-24)

To assist activists in reappropriation of the vigorous and often insistent nature of the psalmists' prayers, I have found it helpful to shout out their words. This helps us enter as fully as possible into the urgent quality of the Psalm's prayer. It may need to be repeated a second time to enable persons to fully join in. The following is a suggestion for using selected portions of Psalm 35 as a vigorous, shared prayer for justice.

"Shouting" the Psalms

1. Introduce the Psalms as a rich source of urgent prayers for social justice, explaining something of their original context.

2. Ask them to use plural pronouns and explain why.

3. Explain also that you will be lining out each line for them to repeat after you (unless you have prepared a copy of the selected verses for each participant).

4. Invite them to stand and shout the following after you. (If they seem too timid, stop and give encouragement to use their full voices.)[5]

> Contend, O God, with those who contend with us;
>> fight against those who fight against us!
> Take hold of shield and buckler,
>> and rise up to help us!
>
> How long, O God, will you look on?
>> Rescue us from their ravages, our lives from the lions!
> You have seen, O God; do not be silent!

> O GOD, DO NOT BE FAR FROM US!
> WAKE UP! BESTIR YOURSELF FOR OUR DEFENSE,
>   FOR OUR CAUSE, OUR GOD AND OUR SOVEREIGN!
>
> DO NOT LET THEM SAY TO THEMSELVES,
>   "AHA, WE HAVE OUR HEART'S DESIRE."
> DO NOT LET THEM SAY, "WE HAVE SWALLOWED YOU UP."
>
> "SHOUT FOR JOY AND BE GLAD, AND SAY EVERMORE,
>   "GREAT IS GOD,
> WHO DELIGHTS IN THE WELFARE OF GOD'S SERVANTS."
>
> THEN OUR TONGUES SHALL TELL OF YOUR RIGHTEOUSNESS
>   AND OF YOUR PRAISE ALL DAY LONG.

5. Now that they have begun to get the idea of it, you might want to
have them repeat the shouting of the prayer-psalm.

6. Following this you might have each person, working individually,
paraphrase the words of the psalm or add his or her own verses,
applying the psalm to a contemporary situation of social injustice.
Those who wish to share their paraphrase could be invited to do
so.

Such appropriation of the Psalms is an example of spiritual practice as resistance. Entering this world of prayer and protest breaks
the bondage of acculturated religion and begins in small but concrete ways to challenge the hegemony of what Walter Wink calls the
Domination System. This sort of prayer is subversion, the voice of a
Christian community caught up in the divine erosion of all hege-
monies. This prayer witnesses to the only true Hegemony, which
dwelt among us humbly as servant and as an agent of anti-hegemony.

Chapter

The Risk of
Faithful
Surrender

Am I willing to accept the grace? Do I lack faith?

A Florida pastor

We are not really prepared to surrender direction of our lives to any thing, power, whatever, other than our own.
Fred, ecumenical staffer in New York

With bold honesty, a Florida pastor raises what may be the most fundamental obstacle of all to our achieving a greater unity of prayer and action: "Do I lack faith?" Certainly, if we do not trust that God is, that God cares, that God is at work in the world, and that God meets us and empowers us and walks with us, then indeed it will make little sense to speak of deepening our spiritual practice alongside our social action.

For most social activists in the church, I suspect that the issue is not so much one of faith versus disbelief as of faith versus half-faith. It may be experienced along the lines of Augustine's "convert me, but not yet"—an inward struggle over a sort of qualified faith: "Yes, God, I'm with you but on my terms, in my own way, and with me pretty much in control."

The issue is sharpened for social activists because engagement with society is a dialectical process involving assertion and forcefulness, on the one hand, and surrender to God, on the other. Most of us probably need to grow in both directions. I certainly stand in need of growth toward greater assertiveness in overtures against injustice, violence, and the rape of creation. At the same time, I also need to grow in surrender to God and in faith in God's working in my life, in those of others, and in the life of social structures. I must join in Fred's confession that "we are not really prepared to surrender direction of our lives to any thing, power, whatever, other than our own."

Spiritual guide Gerald May offers an insightful autobiographical description of an inward conflict familiar to many of us. It deserves quotation at some length:

> All my life I have longed to say yes, to give myself completely, to some Ultimate Someone or Something. I kept this secret for many years because it did not fit the image I wanted to present—that of an independent, self-sufficient man. The desire to surrender myself had been at least partially acceptable when I was a child, but as a man I tried to put away childish things. When I became a physician, and later a psychiatrist, it was still more difficult to admit—even to myself—that something in me was searching for an ultimate self-surrender.
>
> Society, to say nothing of medical and psychiatric training, had taught me to say no rather than yes, to try to determine my own destiny rather than give myself, to seek mastery rather than surrender. For a long time, I tried to believe that I could learn enough and strengthen my will enough to take complete charge of my own life, but it never quite seemed to work.
>
> I remember looking at some of my colleagues once, shortly after my psychiatric training, and feeling deeply disturbed. They appeared to know what they were doing in life. They acted as if they knew what life was all about and how it should be lived, whereas I, in spite of all my education, was filled with more questions and uncertainties than ever.
>
> At one point I even entertained the absurd thought that I perhaps missed some specific chapter in some psychiatric text, the chapter that really explained things. My colleagues appeared to have read it, but somehow I had missed the assignment.

His life's journey, however, finally led him to embrace his yearning for surrender:

> Now I no longer see my desire for self-surrender as a problem. Instead, it seems to be the wellspring of my deepest hope. There is

something in our hearts that calls for a reconciliation of the individual, autonomous qualities of will with the unifying and loving qualities of spirit.

May frames the central issue as one of *willingness* versus *willfulness*:

> Willingness implies a surrendering of one's self-separateness, an entering-into, an immersion in the deepest processes of life itself. It is a realization that one already is a part of some ultimate cosmic process and it is a commitment to participation in that process. In contrast, willfulness is the setting of oneself apart from the fundamental essence of life in an attempt to master, direct, control, or otherwise manipulate existence. More simply, willingness is saying yes to the mystery of being alive in each moment. Willfulness is saying no, or perhaps more commonly, "Yes, but..."[1]

This willingness is a stance of surrender to God that holds the promise to connect us with our true selves and with the Reality of God in our lives and in the world. Yet assertiveness and surrender are inextricably linked. The greater our surrender to God is, the greater our sense of personal power, clarity, and forcefulness will be. Jesus' teaching certainly applies here, "If any want to become my followers, let them deny themselves and take up their cross and follow me. For those who want to save their life will lose it, and those who lose their life for my sake will find it" (Matthew 16:24-25).

In this stance of faith, it makes sense to pray, to place ourselves and our institutional structures within the grace and goodness of God, and to call upon the power of God to redeem individuals and institutions. With such willingness we can persevere in holding to the Jesus vision of partnership, egalitarianism, and reverence for humanity and nature in the midst of the contrary messages, forces, and pressures—even election results—which repeatedly seek to quash such hope.

Activist Frenzy Versus Contemplative Stance

I have found the practice of contemplative prayer to be the most searching and heart-expanding personal spiritual practice in schooling my soul in this willingness. Contemplative prayer is prayer of simple being, of resting before God. It addresses, perhaps as no other form of prayer, what Thomas Merton, the Roman Catholic contemplative-activist, termed our activist frenzy. Hear his searing indictment:

> The rush and pressure of modern life are a form of its innate violence. To allow oneself to be carried away by a multitude of conflicting concerns, to surrender to too many projects, to want to help everyone in everything is to succumb to violence.... The frenzy of the activist... destroys his own inner capacity for peace. It destroys the fruitfulness of his own work, because it kills the root of inner wisdom which makes work fruitful.[2]

This frenzied activism is one of the great practical heresies of our culture. It distinguishes the character of American Christianity and is rampant in my own United Methodist tradition. Doing is so much more important to us than being. Speaking for myself, I often feel that my value depends not only upon what I do, but on my constantly doing something—almost every waking hour. When faced with a social need or issue of injustice, I rush to the question, What can I do? For me, it has led to unnecessary stress and contributed to a chronic physical illness. And so I, and perhaps you too, feel a yearning for a more balanced spirituality, one which includes the contemplative mode, with spaces of quiet, of simple being in the presence of God.

Because contemplative prayer so uniquely addresses and corrects our activist heresy of willful doing, it deserves the special attention of social activists. Until recently, it did not receive very much attention in our churches. As Tilden Edwards explains, the primary modes of spiritual experience in Western Christianity, both Roman Catholic and Protestant, have been the rational and the emotional. Western Christianity can be understood as a tension, sometimes even a battle, between the rational, with its emphasis upon the intellect and ethical reflection, and the emotional, known to American Protestantism particularly through Evangelicalism. Both of these modes serve an important role. But as Edwards points out, there is a third essential mode of spiritual experience that has mostly been missing in Western Christianity, the intuitive or contemplative. It has survived as a sub-tradition in Catholic and Anglican monasteries and in Protestantism primarily through the Quaker tradition; however, for most Western Christians the intuitive, contemplative mode of experiencing God has been undervalued and mostly unnoticed.[3] This contemplative spirituality is today experiencing a renaissance, and there is a growing interest in various forms of contemplative prayer.

Centering Prayer

One basic form of contemplative prayer is centering prayer. It has been promoted in a particularly effective way by Cistercian monk Thomas Keating. This form of contemplation involves the internal repetition of a short mantra-like prayer which fends off distraction and leads the pray-er to "fast" from all thought and images. The invitation is to rest in God with the core of one's being, to be in complete inward nakedness before God, and to surrender even our precious thoughts. For those of us who highly prize knowledge and understanding, this is indeed a profound surrender!

The guidelines are disarmingly (and deceptively) simple:

"1. Choose a sacred word as the symbol of your intention to consent to God's presence and action within.

2. Sitting comfortably and with eyes closed, settle briefly and silently introduce the sacred word as the symbol of your consent to God's presence and action within.

3. When you become aware of thoughts, return ever-so-gently to the sacred word.

4. At the end of the prayer period, remain in silence with eyes closed for a couple of minutes."[4]

Keating recommends that this prayer be practiced twenty to thirty minutes a day.

Becoming Contemplative-Activists

While in the past it has been fashionable to criticize contemplative prayer as inherently anti-activist, leading away from service to humanity, many modern proponents of contemplative prayer find it intrinsically connected to activism and social concern. For them, contemplation and action are related like the inhalation and exhalation of air. One is more inward, the other more outward, but both require each other and are part of the same process. Quaker contemplative Douglas Steere puts it this way:

> Contemplation is not a state of coma, or of religious reverie. If it is genuine prayer, we find our inward life quickened. We sense new directions, or our attention is refocused on neglected ones. We find ourselves being mobilized and our inward resources regrouped in response to the new assignment. We find, in short, that we have been re-enlisted in the redemptive order, that, in these ranks, our former reservations are brushed to one side and a new level of expendability emerges.[5]

Sister Corita Clarke, another advocate of contemplative prayer, insists, "An authentic spirituality summons us to hear especially the cry of the poor and to commit ourselves and our resources in some way to a compassionate response," including to change social structures. In the same vein Henri Nouwen writes:

> Compassion is the fruit of solitude and the basis of all ministry. The purification and transformation that take place in solitude manifest themselves in compassion....In solitude we realize that nothing human is alien to us....In solitude our heart of stone can be turned into a heart of flesh,....a closed heart into a heart that can open itself to all suffering people in a gesture of solidarity.[6]

I find many Christians with deep commitment to social action being drawn toward contemplative prayer and a deeper personal experience of God. They find a sense of rightness in this prayer, a feeling of coming home and fulfilling a secret deep yearning just to be in God. Upon experiencing an introduction to contemplative prayer, one social activist exclaimed, "I've wanted the peace of God all my life, and I never experienced it until now."

A symbol of this growing convergence of prayer and action is W. Paul Jones, a seminary professor of theology for thirty-five years. He took early retirement in order "to become a Family Brother of the Trappist Order, live as a hermit in the Ozark Hills, and quietly try to work with the poor." "Above all," he says, "I am being called by the Spirit to learn simply how to be."[7] Jones has authored *Trumpet at Full Moon*, a remarkably comprehensive compendium of Christian prayer and spiritual practice, which borrows widely from a whole spectrum of traditions, past and present. In this volume there are riches for any serious seeker.

Let me summarize the gifts which many activists discover when embarking upon a deeper life of prayer, especially contemplative prayer:

Ethical Sharpening. In the inner peace of contemplative prayer we can better see things as they are and more clearly recognize the choices before us. We can say a quiet "no" to the attempts of the principalities and powers to seduce our own spirits. As Douglas Steere says, "There is an ethical sharpening that takes place in real Christian prayer which is highly dangerous to any complacency with the order of things as they are."[8]

Capacity to Face the Depths. In the struggle for social justice we sooner or later come to a sense of frustration and impasse. Will things ever change? The forces of reaction and entrenched self-interest seem so powerful. Our own capacities seem so limited, and they are often compromised or misdirected. The standard ways of dealing with such experiences of impasse, according to Sister Constance Fitzgerald, are to minimize the struggle, deny that it is really there, or fall into apathy. She points out, however, that in the life of deep prayer, we can discern in such social impasse the presence of God calling us to conversion, constancy, healing, compassion, and solidarity.[9]

Detachment and Freedom. When we are able to see our social struggle as God's work and can let go of our control and let God lead, we receive the gift of a wonderful detachment from our plans, goals, strategies, and compulsions. This in turn increases our freedom to respond to the special invitations of each moment, both large and small. Our addictive, reactive behavior gets diluted. In our partial disengagement, our effective engagement can be even greater. Such detachment, arising out of surrender in prayer, can enable us to move toward the "nonanxious presence" and sustain the "nonreactive response" which family therapist Edwin Friedman says is necessary to be an effective change agent.[10] In this inner stillness we can become free from any idols we do not wish to serve: the idols of control, arrogance, frenetic activity, taking on too much, and overreaction. By the grace of God we can increasingly say, with the apostle Paul, "It is no longer I who live, but it is Christ who lives in me" (Galatians 2:20).

Empowerment. As we become aware that our being is rooted in God's being and our doing in God's doing, we lay hold of a power of the Holy One "who by the power at work within us is able to accomplish abundantly far more than all we can ask or imagine" (Ephesians 3:20). We come home humbly to our true selves, only to discover that our true selves are united in Christ to a remarkable spiritual-physical network of God-given energy for wholeness. Into the fabric of our person and our concern for human and social redemption are woven the divine power and energy which can enable our action to open life to God's new possibilities.

How do we cultivate this inner stillness? How can we open ourselves to the graces God has in store for us? There can be many ways. One that I have found helpful is the following Breath Prayer for Social Transformation, which is inspired by teachers of breath prayer such as Nancy Roth, Ron del Bene, and Tilden Edwards.

I urge you to experiment with this breath prayer and see if it helps you bring a quality of inner silence to the perplexing issues of your life and social justice ministry. If so, you may want to spend some minutes each day cultivating this sense of inner silence. You could include it with any other daily devotional practice you have, including intercessory prayer, scripture meditation, or body movement. But be sure to allow some open time just to be receptive, open, and attentive to God as God may choose to come to you. At least part of the time allow your gaze to fall gently upon the social issue or institutional challenge with which you are involved. Invite God to enable you to have a long, loving look at it in all its facets. If you are drawn to journaling, you might benefit from regular notations to yourself concerning how God illumines the issue before you. I invite you to regular and intentional practice of inner silence in which to practice the long, loving look at what is Real.

A Breath Prayer for Social Transformation

1. First offer a silent prayer that in this prayer exercise you may be fully present to God. (Without this intentionality the act of prayer may be a hollow shell.)

2. Slowly take in a full breath; then hold your breath for several seconds before slowly exhaling. After exhaling, pause again. Repeat the process over and over again.

3. As you breathe in, consciously breathe into yourself that which is of God; and as you exhale, breathe out of yourself that which is not of God. Let God guide you into any specific content for this prayer, such as breathing in the fruits of the Spirit or breathing out anxiety or the desire to control. Continue for five to ten minutes.

4. Then imagine a specific, problematic situation you face (a social injustice directly confronting you, a challenging meeting, or an abrasive interpersonal relationship). Bring this situation to mind, and as you do so follow the directions in number three above, for another five to ten minutes, breathing into that situation that which is of God and breathing out that not of God. Leave the rest in God's hands.

5. Close your prayer time with your own prayer of thanksgiving and intercession, as you may be led.

6. Finally, record in a journal something of the inner movement you experienced in this prayer time.

Chapter

Discerning the Yearning of God

Meetings are central to performing social action, for it is in meetings that issues are sorted out, critical decisions are made about how the group will face—or avoid—issues, relationships are strengthened, and mutual courage is deepened. But after participating in countless meetings concerning social action, I find myself asking whether we do enough to make space for God in our meetings.

Do not get me wrong. God's presence in our meetings is, of course, not finally dependent upon our allowing space. God is present in human life whenever human beings meet and certainly, we are promised, "where two or three are gathered in [Christ's] name" (Matthew 18:20). We have all been in meetings where, whether God was invoked or not, we felt the palpable presence of God and might have truthfully sung, "Surely, the presence of the Lord is in this place."[1] God's Spirit can move among us in spite of our resistance or inattentiveness.

Nevertheless, our intentionality does make a difference. I don't fully agree with the church executive who assumes, "Of course, God's in our meetings" because "we're a church organization." There is ample evidence that it does matter whether we carry out our meetings with the active intention of allowing space for God. Our receptivity—or resistance—to the Spirit does make a difference. And this difference can be crucial to the faithfulness and effectiveness of our social witness.

Some may experience internal resistance about encouraging an explicit focus on God in our meetings because of negative experiences. Sometimes those who talk most about God seem to be using religion to manipulate people or to promote an oppressive biblical literalism. We have been burned by those who cry "Lord, Lord" but fall far short of following Christ. I share this resistance, and perhaps that is why it has taken me thirty-five years to address this matter! Nevertheless, I am determined not to let the Jerry Falwells and Pat Robertsons shape my spiritual practice, either directly or indirectly. (I am also aware that I too can fall into using the Christian faith to manipulate, to push my agenda, or as a platform for self-righteousness).

Consider two contrasting ways in which we can approach decision making. One is to ask, "What shall we do?" This is a common sense approach, relying more or less upon our own reasoning capacities. The other is to ask, "What is God's yearning for us?" This phrase, which I borrow from Ron del Bene, points to a more intentional focus upon connecting our decision making with God's intention for us, not as if we were robots following a predetermined script, but as ones who intend to "do justice, and to love kindness" as we "walk humbly with [our] God" (Micah 6:8).

I conducted a survey of the national board members of the church-related social action network with which I work. Each represented a regional chapter. I asked them to consider how their chapter tended to frame its decision making and to indicate this on a spectrum. One end of the spectrum represented the question, "What are we going to do?" and the other end, "What is God's yearning for us?"

When the results from all the respondents were collected and averaged, the chapters' ways of framing their decisions were considerably to the end of the spectrum representing the question "What shall we do?" (See point X in the table below). But when I asked these same social action leaders to indicate their own personal way of decision making, their average response was almost exactly as far to the opposite end of the spectrum (see point Y), close to the "What is God's yearning?" pole.

A Comparison of Decision Making Approach Used by Social Action Chapters and Leaders

"What are we/I   "What is God's
going to do?"   yearning for us/me?"

A— — — — —|— — — — —|— — — — —|— — — — —|— — — — —|— — — —–B
          X   Y
Social Action Chapters   Leaders as Individuals

How does one account for the discrepancy? To begin, I believe this informal survey suggests that most Christian social activists as individuals really do want to act according to God's yearning and that they are familiar with historically tested ways of personal devotion for seeking God's yearning: personal prayer, meditation, Bible reading, journaling, trusted conversation, and so forth. But it also suggests that we as social change agents do not have adequate practices, traditions, or common understandings for focusing on "God's yearning for us" in our group decision making.

We simply lack forms of prayer and discernment which relate directly to the decisions we make in our meetings. We need to learn how to address, before God, the obstacles that stand in the way of the group's emptying itself. We need a spiritual praxis that helps clear our corporate receptivity so that God's yearning may be more keenly perceived and acted upon.

In this respect our situation is no different than that of the church as a whole. The church has in many ways adopted the planning and administrative procedures of the business world. There is much to be said for this, of course. The church benefits greatly from sound financial management, careful budgeting, and other responsible business practices. Management by objectives, goal setting, needs assessment and problem-solving techniques can be and are used by God to help churches be faithful stewards of their resources. In the process, however, the church may be neglecting some of its unique gifts for decision making.

I sense a growing desire for our actions as justice-seekers to spring more intentionally from the moving of God's Spirit in our meetings.

Here are some fundamental assumptions about God's intentions for our social change meetings, based on ones articulated by Tilda Norberg and Robert D. Webber. They provide the foundation for a greater degree of spiritual discernment in these meetings:[2]

- *The group is called by God to a prophetic ministry* of promoting the justice, peace, and reconciliation for which God yearns, both within and beyond the church. As the Franciscans have said so well, we are called to "look at what is happening in the world from the perspective of the poor, in fellowship with all those considered unimportant."[3]

- *God cares about our mission, even in details* such as who takes leadership positions, what issues and strategies we choose, and how to provide the resources of time, money, and people power. God is a loving God and knows even more about our needs than we do.

- *Surrender to God's yearning for us is not "giving up" but "giving over."* We remain fully engaged even as we surrender. The wisdom of God is discerned through the process of *giving over* our agenda to God with openness to any surprising new direction.

- *God passionately loves us*, yearns for the best for us, and wants to communicate with us. Despite the static in our communication lines to God we trust that God is nevertheless able to get through to us.

- *Discernment is seeking God's yearning* about what to pray for and what action to take.

While it is conceivable that our active trust in God is so much a part of us and our group that no further cultivation of such trust is necessary in our meetings, this is highly unlikely. As human beings, we are all subject to wandering minds and hearts, characterological compulsions, denial, impulses to take on either too much or too little, and fear and anxiety, especially when risks become apparent.

These can be compounded in group meetings in which one person's limitation compounds that of another. Given these realities, I believe that intentional cultivation of our deep trust in God is essential.

Enveloping a Meeting in Prayer

Cultivating a trust in God along the lines of the above assumptions will do much to transform our meetings and to make intentional space for God in them. Here are some suggestions for the preparation and conduct of a meeting:

- Pray for the meeting ahead of time. Where possible, let several persons gather in advance to pray, ideally in the meeting space itself. If circumstances do not allow this, the prayer can be done individually and in some other place, but with a keen imaging of the meeting space and participants.

- Pray that the meeting space and those about to gather for the meeting be cleared of any impediment to the free moving of the Holy Spirit. Reverently image the presence of God as light (or wind, music, wisdom, or another personal image of God) moving through the entire space and enveloping each person about to gather. This kind of prayer can be done moving throughout the room, consciously sitting or standing at the places persons are about to occupy, imaging each in the light of God.

- Prepare in advance for a devotional time during the meeting and assure that it is done thoughtfully, with a specific view to enabling meeting participants to lay aside other concerns and focus on discerning God's yearning. Plan to employ any formal prayer time to lift up the particular agenda of the meeting, invite God's active presence, and call participants to faith in God's loving care for the details of the meeting.

- Consider having one participant act as intercessor at all times during the meeting. This could be one particular person who withdraws from the business of the entire meeting to pray for its clarity and focus. Or the intercessor role could be passed from one person to another throughout the meeting. In this shared intercession model, you should have a symbol to pass among the participants. A Salvadoran cross works well, but almost any small object will do. Each person keeps it for ten to fifteen minutes while praying on behalf of the meeting. Then it is passed on to the next person. If you are not ready for your turn when the cross comes to you, you simply pass it and take your turn the next time around.

- When a particularly challenging issue comes up, call for a time of discernment in which the yearning of God is explicitly sought for the issue at hand. Essentially this means taking some time of silence in order to

  a) invite God into the problem;

  b) seek simply to sit in God's presence, ignoring all the ideas and chatter in our own heads;

  c) pay attention to what arises within each one (scripture verses, images, memories, physical sensations, or plans of action), trusting that what does arise is God's way of working in us;

  d) share what emerges for each; and finally

  e) explore any emerging direction through prayer and discussion.[4]

- As the Spirit moves you, you might develop a common breath prayer for the group, to be practiced silently throughout the meeting. For instance, the group could adopt as its own the sentence, "*Gracious God* (on the inhalation), *be with us* (on the exhalation)." Or "*Let justice roll down* (on the inhalation) *like waters* (on the exhalation)." The common use of such a prayer can be a powerful way to "pray without ceasing."[5]

Those who have used such prayers as these report that they are inwardly changed and that amazing things can happen at the meetings. People are enabled to reframe their perspective on the meeting and often find themselves with a new inner quiet. In one instance a social action organization was led to new confidence and insight regarding how to meet the burden of its financial needs. In another case the sharing out of the silence helped a meeting participant hear in a fresh way how women were being hurt by the blanket condemnations of the Re-Imagining Conference on women and theology. Almost universally, this intentionality yields a sense of deep peace.[6]

Factoring Justice into Discernment

I want to stress the importance of sensitivity to justice issues in the process of spiritual discernment. Regrettably, in the revival of attention to discernment, the peace and justice dimension is quite often absent.

Sensitivity to justice issues simply cannot be assumed in any Christian discernment process. As we have discussed, we North American Christians live in a basically hostile situation dominated by consumerism, free market ideology, antigovernment prejudice, and rampant individualism. Socially sensitive attitudes are ridiculed as "p.c." or "politically correct." Compassion and justice are sacrificed as too costly. To ignore the justice question is to encourage individualist decisions that easily accept antijustice prejudices. Fortunately, much careful thinking is being done to provide tools for awareness of social location (the personal or group interests which we have by virtue of our gender, race, ethnicity, class, nationality, physical capacities, or age) in discernment.

I cannot emphasize enough the shortcomings of the individualistic approach to discernment. The process of making faithful decisions is seriously compromised when performed without reference to justice concerns. Take, for instance, a recent book by Danny Morris, as vigorous a promoter of the use of spiritual discernment as one could find. His workbook on discernment contains many helpful suggestions to enable individuals and groups to proceed step-by-step in a discernment process. His approach is ecumenical in scope, highlighting both the Ignatian model of discernment and the Quaker tradition of assembling a committee of clearness.[7] However, no guideline is offered that encourages reflection upon one's social-economic context in the light of what God is doing. Quaker John Woolman's witness against slavery is mentioned but only tangentially. Justice questions are simply bypassed.

A Formal Discernment Process

Faithful decisions require that we ask whose interests are being served. Those committed to the whole gospel need to be intentional about the contextual and justice-related aspects of decision making. For this reason I have been particularly excited to discover a detailed form of discernment process which gives this kind of guidance, the Prayer-Action Cycle.[8] This process was first introduced to me by the Center for Spirituality and Justice while I was guiding a strategy to secure the participation of a denominational pension board in the burgeoning movement for economic sanctions against South Africa. I worked through the cycle with a spiritual guide and found it yields surprising and grace-filled results.

In using this process I discovered how I, like the church board, was caught up in a Spirit of Fear and Arrogance. It also helped me realize that in spite of our differences with the board, my fellow petitioners and I were coming to a point of care and compassion for the board and its members, even those most opposed to change. With the help of this process, the social transformation question gradually reframed itself as "How do we love this board into change?" I found a new freedom in living that question. This experience will be discussed further in a later chapter.

Church action groups to which I have introduced the Prayer-Action Cycle have found it quite helpful. In one case, a concerned pastor in California was frustrated with the continued resistance of her congregation to any kind of mission involvement beyond the walls of the church. She had decided it was hopeless and had concluded she would ask for a change of assignment when the yearly appointment time came around. After she spent a day with the Prayer-Action Cycle, however, God led her to an awareness of some new possibilities and a new sense of hope for that congregation. She decided that God wanted her to continue ministry there.

As you can see from the accompanying text of the Prayer-Action Cycle, there are four basic movements: awareness, social analysis, faith reflection, and action. These are the steps we generally go through in generating any faith-based action, whether in an instant or over a longer period. Take, for instance, a situation in which you see a child run out in front of an oncoming car. Here all four aspects are completed almost instantaneously: (1) you *become aware* of the child going out into the street and are moved by compassion; (2) you instantaneously *analyze* the situation and conclude that the child is in great danger; (3) you are *prompted by your faith conviction* that the life and well-being of the child is sacred to God; and, (4) you immediately *leap into action* and dash into the street to rescue the child.

The Prayer-Action Cycle lifts up for our careful scrutiny each movement of the cycle, to ensure that we bring intentionality and a justice lens to each aspect in the light of our faith commitment. Note that each phase is to be entered into prayerfully, asking God to grant the gift of discernment. In effect, the entire process is a faith reflection process, although this is more explicit in the third phase.

The **Awareness Phase** is intended to sharpen our sensitivity to the totality of the situation. The questions seek to bring to light elements of which we might not be fully aware. You are encouraged to identify your feelings and name what is at stake for you in the issue at hand, what your personal interests are. You are also invited to name the poor and oppressed, relative to your issue. Thus the justice dimension is raised right at the beginning. Persons generally find it especially illuminating to reflect on whom they tend to leave out of consideration. For example, this can bring into awareness generations yet to come, potential victims, or other individuals on the periphery of your considerations.

The **Social Analysis Phase** very directly probes the historical, social, and power issues at stake. Persons often find the question about operative assumptions quite revealing, for this uncovers the unwritten, hidden assumptions which often are the source of obstacles to change.[9] The question about seeds of new life probes the sources for hope and begins to awaken awareness of God's redemptive activity in the situation.

The **Faith Reflection Phase** urges you to measure the situation explicitly in relation to your faith commitments. It begins, like a worship service, with thanksgiving to God. The question about what memory is awakened of an event in Christ's life, or of a particular scripture passage, usually turns out to be very fruitful. People tend to be surprised by what emerges for them. The phase closes by probing the openings to God and incipient transformations present in the situation.

In the concluding **Action Phase** the openings and turnings to God are further reflected upon and specific action alternatives named. Discernment is invited and the criterion of inner freedom introduced. You are urged to indicate how the results of a decided-upon action would be evaluated. Finally, prayer for strength and courage is summoned.

The Prayer-Action Cycle can be used in a variety of ways. If there is sufficient time, your group could devote a whole meeting to each movement of the cycle. Or an overnight retreat could be scheduled so as to move through the whole cycle in one concentrated experience. When there is less time, a certain few of the questions could be selected for group members to meditate on between meetings. Other questions could be used as the basis for the devotions at a given meeting. The cycle offers a potentially inexhaustible source for reflection in the Spirit. Every time an action has been taken, or any new events have taken place, the situation changes; the cycle of Awareness-Analysis-Faith Reflection-Action begins again.

I have found that there are two critical conditions that need to be met in order for the Prayer-Action Cycle to be helpful. Users must be clear about the issue or situation they are discerning. If there is fuzziness in this respect, then the results are also likely to be fuzzy and perhaps frustrating. For instance, a person or group may feel troubled about how hard it is for youth to grow up today. But unless persons can identify a particular aspect of the pressures upon youth, the Prayer-Action Cycle is not likely to be of much help. Once a concrete issue is identified, such as the lack of meaningful work, then the Cycle may be helpful. If there is an insurmountable lack of clarity, then that lack of clarity itself should be chosen as the focus issue.

The Prayer-Action Cycle

I. Awareness Phase

Pray for the light to know which of your feelings and thoughts are promptings of the Holy Spirit.

a. What is happening and with whom have you identified in relation to the issue?

b. How do you find yourself responding—in (1) behavior, (2) feelings, and (3) prayer?

c. What is your personal stake in the issue?

d. Who are the poor and oppressed, relative to this institution and context?

e. When you consider this issue, are there any people or groups you tend to leave out?

f. With whom do you lack personal relationships?

II. Social Analysis Phase

Pray that you may recognize the "signs of the times" (in a biblical sense) and the sources of creativity and hope.

a. What are the traditions and history surrounding this issue and the institution(s) involved?

b. What are the operative assumptions?

c. What are the social relations (class, race, gender, and so forth) involved?

d. How is power being exercised? Who makes decisions? Who benefits? Who bears a cost?

e. What will happen if the situation continues as it is now?

f. Are there any seeds of new life?

g. What relationships do you have with key persons? With whom do you need to build relationships?

III. Faith Reflection Phase

Pray to be aware of the reality and presence of God in this situation.

a. For what in this situation ought one to offer thanks to God?

b. What are the gospel values and church social teachings that relate to the situation?

c. What theological affirmations are involved?

d. As you reflect prayerfully about the issue being considered, what event in Christ's life or scripture passage emerges for you?

e. What turns away from God? What is sinful regarding this issue? What forces of evil seem to be at work?

f. In what way have you turned from God in this situation?

g. What is opening to God? What is graced in this situation?

h. Have there been any conversion or transformation in your experience with this process so far? Any insights or understandings? Any turning to God?

IV. Action Phase

Pray to discern the best course of action.

a. Did any concrete actions suggest themselves to you during the Faith Reflection?

b. What are the action alternatives you can identify?

c. Which of them would be most effective? Which seem to arise most clearly out of, or lead to, an inner freedom?

d. In what way does the power of God need especially to be invoked? How can this be done?

e. Who would be involved in carrying out the action?

f. What means will be used to evaluate this action?

Pray for the strength and courage to move into the decisions and actions that have emerged.

Further, it is important that the group or individual using the Cycle connect the issue to their own lives. However laudable, choosing world hunger as a general focus may not be very fruitful. Much better is: "How can I help my local church to be involved in alleviating world hunger?" or "How can I improve the effectiveness of the board of the feeding program of which I am member?" Again, if one cannot be that specific, the person might well use the Cycle to ask God's guidance in discerning a specific arena of activity. The central question would then be: "How do I/we actually do something specific about our concern for world hunger?"

The fruitfulness of the Prayer-Action Cycle for discernment is illustrated by the report of Susan, a clergywoman seeking to discern a new shape to her ministry:

I knew God was calling me to a new justice ministry related to spiritual formation and inner healing. However, I had no idea what form this new ministry should take. Applying the Prayer-Action discernment cycle cleared away the mist and brought a clear vision into focus. The final result was the establishment of Open Door Ministries, a healing prayer and retreat ministry which I designed and to which I was appointed.... I've also used the discernment process in group settings, to discover how to pray in various justice-related situations, such as in a newly designed spiritual formation program for prison inmates, and when sexual misconduct charges are brought against people in our judicatory.

In another instance, the Prayer-Action Cycle provided the occasion for Joanne, an active lay leader, to take a significant step in a life-changing process. She describes in these words the impact of her experience of the Prayer-Action Cycle in a group retreat emphasizing one's calling to social ministry:

The issue I was led to focus on was how I could effectively advocate for the mentally ill or the families of the mentally ill.

At that time I was coming from an abusive congregation into a very loving congregation but did not trust anyone with the secrets of my daughter's mental illness.... Through the steps of the discernment process, I was led to know that someday I would be able to speak openly about mental illness and how it was affecting my own family. That time finally came four months later when I began to speak about mental illness in Sunday school classes. I am constantly amazed at how much easier it is becoming to speak frankly to people and how others with similar problems are then prompted to speak frankly with me. Rather than a silent sufferer, I now am a useful "family member," an effective member of the Alliance for the Mentally Ill.

Later she was led to write some meditations on the Stations of the Cross regarding the impact of mental illness on families.

The Cycle's fruitfulness for group discernment has been demonstrated in a series of ten meetings with aggrieved tenants in the South Bronx, New York City. As part of their church's ministry, the organizers met with some fifteen tenants about their very serious concerns for building security. Drug traffickers would loiter in the buildings, with building security personnel claiming they were a police problem and the police contending they were a building security matter. In the Social Analysis phase the tenants, coached by the organizers, discovered that the ownership of the buildings was not in the hands of the building managers, as they had been told, but of absentee landowners in Boston.

The Faith Reflection phase was especially interesting since only two of the tenants were church-going Christians, and the remainder were Muslim, humanist, lapsed Christian, or totally unconnected religiously. The organizers were able, though, to assist the tenants in connecting their struggle to whatever were their core beliefs, whether found in the Koran, poetry, the Bible, or their fundamental convictions about human decency, fairness, and justice. Throughout the ten-week process the organizers equipped the tenants with new skills for asserting their rights. One of the culminating actions was to arrange a personal confrontation with the building owners, forcing the owners to assume direct responsibility for building security.

Each action was evaluated, and the new situation again assessed in terms of the Prayer-Action Cycle. The momentum continued after the ten-week period of direct guidance by the organizers, and the tenants went on to organize a tenants' organization.

Chapter

Spiritual Struggle with the Powers

This is spiritual warfare!
                    A Florida pastor

Take no part in the unfruitful works of darkness, but instead expose them.
                    Ephesians 5:11

A pastor in Florida was describing to me what it was like in Florida dealing with the inordinate power of the Religious Right. Spontaneously she blurted out, "This is spiritual warfare, and we need to be involved."

I was a bit startled, for the term "spiritual warfare" is usually used by religious conservatives, rather than those like her who challenge their political agenda. We know what damage a crusade mentality can do, and we are well aware of how religiously inspired visions of the good have engendered endless wars and strife among Christians themselves, right down to the present strife between Catholic Republicans and Protestant Loyalists in Northern Ireland. On a personal level we know too well how easily a Christian view of struggle against evil can lead to a self-righteousness that is the antithesis of a genuine Christian spirit. Furthermore, it seems that generally those who most avidly espouse a view of spiritual warfare raise the political banner of Christ for an agenda that promotes oppression and serves the status quo.

Yet in the New Testament the vocabularies of warfare and, to a lesser degree, athletic contest provide the primary images describing the inner and outer struggles of Jesus' followers. Jesus and the early believing community recognized that they were engaged with God in a struggle against everything opposed to God. The phrase in the Jesus prayer is explicit: "Deliver us from evil." At the root of human life is a cosmic drama between God and power opposed to God, variously called Satan, Beelzebub, the strong man, or evil.

The earliest Christian confession was a declaration of spiritual war against the ultimate claims of empire, empire-religion, and all forms of oppression. "Jesus Christ is Lord" or "Jesus Christ is Sovereign" meant that Jesus, not Caesar, was the final authority whom Christians served. This confession was a life-and-death matter, for those serving Caesar were very jealous of their power and extremely sensitive to any hint of a threat to it.

A basic question for us is whether peace or conflict is the normal state of human life. I suspect that our inclination to believe that lack of conflict is normal has more to do with our relatively comfortable upbringing and the middle-class interest in stability (that is, our social location) than it has to do with biblically based faith.

I believe we Christian activists who know Jesus as Liberator and harbinger of justice ignore the concept of spiritual struggle at considerable peril. We have essentially left the field of spiritual conflict to those serving the status quo in the name of Christ. A conflict-as-normative worldview better corresponds both to experience and the biblical account than a peace-as-normative view. We must reclaim the vision of spiritual conflict against evil, but in the spirit of the "Lord" Jesus who interpreted sovereignty as suffering servanthood. Only thus will we have a conceptual framework for the unique and bold kind of ministry to which the church is called.

Jesus' ministry was based on an understanding that there is a fundamental conflict between God's way and the way of "the world." Jesus operated out of a conflict model of reality and an insistence that his followers join him in a divine engagement. "No one can serve two masters," he declared, "for a person who is enslaved will either hate the one and love the other, or be devoted to the one and despise the other" (Matthew 6:24).

To express the basic metaphor I prefer the term "spiritual struggle" to "spiritual warfare"—hoping to temper the language of war yet convey the sense of vigorous, disciplined conflict between God and those powers that work against God. I would also urge a careful and faithful use of other biblical terminology, whether from the world of athletics or warfare. We cannot give up for instance, the language of Ephesians 6 ("Put on the whole armor of God...."), but we must always make clear that in Christ our very vocabulary may be transformed in meaning. The Jesus community took the political language of domination and turned it upside down. Jesus was named "prince," but "of peace," not domination. His lordship was a servanthood, in which he "emptied Christ's self, taking the form of a servant" (Philippians 2:7). We stand in a powerful tradition of transforming the meaning of borrowed vocabulary.

If the church operated more out of a conflict model of reality, perhaps pastors and church leaders would not have such trouble dealing with conflict in our churches. As it is, the operative eleventh commandment is "Do not rock the boat." We also tend to shy away from engagement in social conflict in the community. When engagement is made, too often we church leaders want to go in as reconcilers and mediators between two sides rather than to discern how justice is to be served and enter on the side of justice.

The Anatomy of the Powers

What then is the nature of this conflict in which we as activist Christians are engaged? Who, or what, is the enemy? What are we up against when we confront oppression in all its forms, when we struggle with "the powers of sin and death"?

I cannot overemphasize that from a Christian viewpoint the enemy with which we are engaged in spiritual conflict is not individuals as such, not even political figures, nor human institutions as such. Rather it is the spiritual force of evil which bends individual wills and institutional functioning to its purposes. In Christian baptismal vows we rightly renounce "the spiritual forces of wickedness" and "the evil powers of this world."

Walter Wink has done a marvelous service to Christian activists in describing the anatomy of evil in terms of both New Testament language and social analysis. Each book in his trilogy on the powers richly rewards close study by Christian social activists.[1] The work has begun to have its deserved impact, especially since the publication in 1992 of the capstone volume *Engaging the Powers: Discernment and Resistance in a World of Domination*. Wink's work opens new vistas for biblically grounded spiritual praxis in a justice-seeking context. Two of his concepts are particularly important as basic building blocks for the spirituality of justice action.

The first is his understanding of the biblical conception of "the powers." The powers are not, as some would have it, ethereal, noncorporal entities. Nor is the biblical language about principalities and powers to be simply reduced to denoting human institutions and structures. The powers are both material and spiritual, with both an outer and an interior aspect. Hence his formula: $p = o + i$, that is, **powers = outer manifestation + inner spirituality.**

I find this formulation to be quite helpful to Christian activists. They readily recognize the **outer manifestations** of institutions and structures, those aspects which can be measured and observed with the five senses. And when led to think about it, activists recognize that the institutions we come up against do have an **inner spirituality,** an intrinsic way of doing things, with allegiances, loyalties, and histories which shape their choices and mold their inner disposition for being in the world. This interiority endures despite changes in personnel and leadership, or in rules and policies. Activists know intuitively that in the struggle for justice "our struggle is not against enemies made of blood and flesh [that is, not with institutions only in their outer form] but against the rulers, against the authorities, ... against the spiritual forces of evil [entities with both an outer form and an inner spirituality]" (Ephesians 6:12).

Recognizing the spirituality of institutions is of central significance to Christian social activists because it opens the way for us to claim our vocation as religious change agents. We have a special vocation as those who are called by the Spirit to address not only the outward, physical aspects (budgets, leaders, members, policies, buildings, and so forth) of wayward institutions, but also their inner spirituality (customs, attitudes, allegiances, self-image, and such). We are called to nothing less than interceding for the souls of institutions.

The inner spirituality of institutions often turns toward idolatry. Rejecting their God-given vocation of serving the common good, they serve idolatrous ends, such as greed, self-preservation, and image-polishing. Like everything in our capitalist culture, institutions are under constant pressure to serve the consumerist way of life and the classist, racist, patriarchal power structures which sustain it. As some veteran community activists say, institutions, when left to their own ends, "eat people."

Our economic institutions serve the idols of survival and profit. This perverted inner spirituality leads directly to their abusive behavior: contempt for the human consequences of corporate takeovers, abandonment of the communities to which they have long been indebted, exploitation of human beings as workers, aggressive marketing of commodities known to be harmful, and the despoliation of creation. "The principalities' radical anxiety about survival," concludes Bill Wylie Kellerman, "is in fact their homage to death."[2]

A dramatic example of a specific idolatrous institution that eats people is the prison system in Venezuela, declared in June 1994 by a visiting delegation to be "the most dangerous in Latin America."[3] Even the outward manifestations, the measurable data, were appalling. Prisons were packed with three times their capacity of prisoners. Prison administrators failed to keep track of prisoners' records, and many who should have been released were held indefinitely. As James Brooke wrote in the *New York Times*, "Feeling increasingly cornered by crime, Venezuela quietly follows a policy of locking up the suspects and virtually throwing away the key. According to the Justice Ministry, only 40 percent of Venezuela's prisoners have been tried. The rest await trial, a process that can take up to five years."[4]

In the Catia Prison of Caracas, the scene evoked for the reporter was of an eighteenth-century slave ship: 150 listless men packed shoulder-to-shoulder in a cell twenty yards long by four yards wide. In one cell block, there were 5 men crowded into each cell, with 344 men for one bathroom. The prison budget limited expenditures to about fifty cents a day per inmate. Despite Venezuela's position as one of Latin America's most affluent nations and despite severe criticism for overcrowding, Venezuela's proposed 1995 budget actually cut prison spending by 17 percent.

It is hard to glean the inner spirituality of this prison system from a news report, but some of its elements can be inferred. There is a long tradition of nightmarish prison conditions in Latin America, beginning with Spanish rule. Mary Eva Caguaripano, prison coordinator for Provea, Venezuela's leading human rights group, said, "The national government insists on treating the jail problem as an image problem. What most worries them is the bad image overseas."[5] This would constitute a high level of denial, callousness, and contempt for the human lives of the prisoners. Prisoners' lives were considered cheap and expendable. In a November 1992 breakout attempt, most of the sixty-three inmates who died were shot in the back. Corruption was endemic, with prisoners selling mattresses for drugs. A conspiracy of silence prevailed, and even prisoners felt compelled to be silent about what went on inside. Meanwhile growing fear of crime, which had surged as living standards plunged in preceding years, had increased the callousness of the general population toward the prisoners' plight. In the language of the powers, we could infer this much: the Catia prison was possessed by the Spirit of Contempt toward life; the populace was in the grip of the Spirit of Fear; and the government was embracing the Spirit of Denial regarding prison conditions.

The other key to Wink's understanding of the powers is that simultaneously

> The powers are good,
> The powers are fallen,
> The powers can be redeemed.[6]

The powers are *good*. All things are created in, through, and for Christ, including the powers as social structures (Colossians 1:16). Institutions are required for human existence. Without subsystems carrying out functions for economic life, public safety, raising of children, health care, and more, human life would be impossible. But Wink offers a caution:

> We must be careful here. To assert that God created the Powers does not imply that God endorses any particular Power at any given time. God did not create capitalism or socialism, but there must be some

kind of economic system. The simultaneity of creation, fall, and redemption means that God at one and the same time *upholds* a given political or economic system, since some such system is required to support human life; *condemns* that system insofar as it is destructive of full human actualization; and *presses for its transformation* into a more humane order. Conservatives stress the first, revolutionaries the second. (67)

At the same time all the powers are *fallen*. Though destined and intended to serve God and the general welfare, they fall short of this calling. The Venezuelan prison system exists in extraordinary denial of the general welfare and dignity of human beings and therefore is idolatrous and against God. Wink gives some examples closer to home:

> An institution may place its own good above the general welfare. A corporation may cut corners on costs by producing defective products that endanger lives. Union leadership may become more preoccupied with extending its personal advantages than fighting for better working conditions for the rank and file. (67)

We could add many more examples, such as neighborhood associations that become un-neighborly toward strangers and fall into the NIMBY ("not in my backyard") syndrome, or police departments, intended to protect all, that only protect some while preying upon others.

To acknowledge that the powers are fallen is to take an unvarnished, realistic view of reality. Whether we want to face it or not, brute evil exists. In spite of our fancies, hopes, and delusions, radical evil takes place. A male nurse rapes postoperative female patients while they are still under anesthesia. Staff of a city-owned shelter for battered women demand sex of the women and allow their abusers into the shelter at night. Satanic cults force children to murder babies. Persons in positions of sacred trust violate that trust. Torture is systematically employed by regimes to hold populations in subjugation. In secret our own government curries favor and manipulates foreign governments. Ten of the 127 prisoners killed in a Venezuelan prison riot in January 1994 should not have even been in jail at that point, but prison administrators had lost their release orders.

Again a caution from Wink:

> The Fall does not revoke the gift of life, or the vocation to live
> humanly in the midst of a fallen creation. The Fall does not mean that
> everything we do is evil, vain, or hopeless, but merely that it is all
> ambiguous, tainted with egocentricity, subject to deflection from its
> divine goal, or capable of being co-opted toward other ends. All that
> distinguishes Christians is the confidence that we have been recon-
> ciled with God in the very midst of a fallen world. (73)

Finally, the powers can also be *redeemed*. God is involved in a continuing process of restitution, "neutralizing their proclivity to evil,"
which enables them in some way to act selflessly, to work genuinely
for the common good. There are "moments of lucidity," Wink says,
"when a subsystem offers itself to the whole" (70). Even though it is
fragmentary, a sense of harmonious unity can be tasted now.

It is difficult to imagine how the Venezuelan prison system is
being redeemed by God. Yet we believe in God's continuing work to
neutralize even this system's proclivity to evil. The continued monitoring by the Venezuelan human rights group is one example of this.
God acts by stripping the veil of silence and secrecy from evil. The
coverage by the *New York Times* and the recent world exposé by
Amnesty International are further steps in embarrassing Venezuelan
officials. We can trust that these exposés are an opening for other
interventions by those who are the caring hands of God.

When Toys 'R' Us, Sears, Target, and K-Mart retail chains
stopped selling toy guns that could be modified to look like real
guns, these powers experienced some measure of redemption. When
Women in Distress of Broward County, which operates Florida's
largest and oldest shelter for abused women, arranged for four members of the Miami Dolphins professional football team to talk can-
didly about their experiences with abuse of women, God's activity of
redemption could be glimpsed.

In the fall 1994 season of unusually vitriolic and cynical political
campaigning, the campaign of Bob Massie, the Democratic candidate for lieutenant governor of Massachusetts, stood out as a sign of
redemptive possibility. Massie, an Episcopal priest and Harvard
Divinity School teacher, ran a "losing" campaign for lieutenant gov-

ernor in Massachusetts which became a sign of what humanizing political races might be. Infected with HIV fifteen years ago through blood transfusions to treat his hemophilia (he had 496 transfusions between the ages of six and twelve), Massie ran a low cost, no-frills campaign that featured speaking from the heart. According to one deeply moved young person, he gave people "hope that things could actually turn out for the good." Massie credits Nelson Mandela and Vaclav Havel with inspiring him to believe that "tremendous new things can take place."[7] His campaign won widespread admiration and caused observers to express regret that someone like him had no possibility of winning the election in the present political climate. In losing, Massie's campaign became a sign that the powers of politics can be redeemed.

The three dimensions of the powers, Wink insists, are experienced simultaneously:

> A given Power can and, at one time or another, probably does manifest all three aspects simultaneously: it performs a necessary function and is created in, through, and for Christ; it is fallen; and it may experience moments when it becomes transparent to the purposes for which it was created. It is possible, right in the midst of the old reality, for both people and Powers to live in relative emancipation from the power of death. (70)

When we understand this inner spirituality of the powers, our Christian ministry to them is self-evident. It is to remind them of the goodness of their creation, of the good ends to which they were created, and to open the way for God's redemption of them.

> Nothing is outside the redemptive care and transforming love of God. The Powers are not intrinsically evil; they are only fallen. What sinks can be made to rise again. We are freed, then, from the temptation to satanize the perpetrators of evil. We can love our nation or church or school, not blindly, but critically, recalling it to its own highest self-professed ideals and identities. We can challenge these institutions to live up to the vocation that is theirs by virtue of their sheer createdness. We can oppose their actions while honoring their necessity.

For example, a factory is polluting the water and air of our city, and we want it cleaned up. We can engage in that struggle knowing that its employees need jobs, and that their families are also at risk from the pollution, just as ours are. We can talk without hatred to the hard-nosed representatives of the plant, because we know that they, and we, and this factory, are encompassed by the love of God, and exist to serve the One in and through and for whom we were all created. We do not have to struggle to bring this plant into the orbit of God's system. It is already there. We have only to remind its managers that it exists to serve values beyond itself (though this "reminding" may require a protracted boycott or strike). (68)

Our social ministry is the pastoral task of participating with God in the redemption of the institutional powers, reclaiming them for their divine vocation. In the next chapter we discuss how we may go about such a ministry.

Chapter

Liberating
Christian
Ritual for
Social
Transform-
ation

For our struggle is not against enemies made of blood and flesh, but against the rulers, against the authorities, against the cosmic powers of this present evil age....
Ephesians 6:12

Much of Christian ritual has served to bless the status quo, especially since Emperor Constantine made Christianty the religion of the empire. The pressure upon the church to provide public legitimation and blessing for the powers-that-be remains enormous. When I was a young pastor in my first year, I was asked to give the prayer at the annual Flag Day ceremony in the close-knit, conservative community served by the church I pastored. At the time, United States military involvement in Vietnam was rapidly escalating, patriotic fervor was building, and the American flag had been claimed by war supporters as the symbol of their cause. I recall the great ambivalence with which I offered that public prayer and the pains I took to make it a prayer for peace in a time of war. Whether that justified my participation I am still not sure, for I was engaging in an essentially Constantinian act by offering prayer at a ceremony celebrating the symbols of a nation engaged in what I believed to be an unjust war. Richard Rohr underscores the inherent contradiction, "Religion has been co-opted to legitimize and bless the selfish interests of the ruling class, while still daring to pray to the poor man Jesus, and still daring to read his sermons in our churches."[1]

As far back as the writing of the New

Testament, a conservative tendency has been at work accommodating the gospel to structures of domination. Over time, the memory of Jesus' discipleship of equals among women and men was forgotten, and the New Testament church came more and more under the exclusive leadership of men, as is especially evident in the Pastoral Epistles.[2]

By the third century C.E. the worship of Roman emperors had become well established and served, in Wink's words, "to expose the acids eating at the fabric of empire. Anyone suspected of revolutionary designs or subversive thoughts could be required to burn a pinch of incense before the emperor's image, and refusal was punishable by death."[3]

Throughout most of Christian history, especially after Constantine the Great's merging of Christianity and empire, the church has been happy to burn a pinch of incense before the political and economic powers-that-be. All too infrequently in Christian history do we find the church enacting public liturgy to challenge entrenched structural evil.

A new era of public spiritual practice for our time was ushered in by the African American church in the United States during the Civil Rights movement of the 1950s and 1960s. The urgency of the times, the deep Christian roots among southern blacks (shared in many ways by the dominant white culture), the justice tradition in African American Christianity, and the emergence of charismatic leaders like Martin Luther King, Jr. and Fannie Lou Hamer all fed the development of a remarkable new tradition of public Christian ritual.

Civil rights demonstrations typically began in the church building with the singing of hymns and freedom songs (often synonymous), preaching, testifying, prayer, and collection of an offering. Through this the oppressed people of God laid claim to God's power in the struggle against the powers of evil in the community, "against the rulers, against the authorities, against the cosmic powers of this present evil age" (Ephesians 6:12). They clearly identified these evil powers as racial segregation and those instruments that buttressed it—the economic, political, and social powers-that-be, as well as the white religious power structure.

Imbued with the Spirit of God, this ad hoc congregation then emptied out onto the streets, where, in effect, the church service continued, though now in an alien land, with the police power of the segregated society monitoring, blocking, and confronting the people of God on the march to "freedomland." The fervent singing continued, passionate prayer was offered, and in the very act of defying the authorities the cross of Christ was taken up. The sidewalks, the streets, and the city hall were claimed for the Reign of God, in which there would be "black and white together." Standing before the courthouse, the city hall, or the jail, the people of God made visible the moral claim of Christ to the earthly instruments of power that had surrendered themselves to false idols.

Usually the march laid moral claim to unsegregated use of public facilities, employment opportunities, or voting rights. Frequently those laying the divine claim upon these institutions were arrested and jailed. In the process song and prayer continued to express the declaration that all institutions exist, not to be the oppressive tools of systemic evil, but to serve the humanizing work of God in history.[4] Time and time again the jails were filled with hundreds singing "Ain't nobody gonna turn me 'round," "Keep your eyes on the prize," and "Let my people go."

"A Liturgy of the Social Gospel"

The ritual actions of these Christians declared a Word whose power was both spiritual and physical. A relatively small band of Christians ignited and sustained a movement for racial justice, the powerful effects of which are evident down to this day. Racial segregation was convincingly delegitimated. Through the Civil Rights movement of African Americans, all sectors of society received an education in nonviolent protest action. Most important for our purposes, sectors of the church were set free to take the church to the streets, courthouses, and city halls of the land. The social liturgical tradition born in the Civil Rights movement has been nurtured through subsequent social movements, including the mostly Roman Catholic farm worker movement under Cesar Chavez, the interfaith anti-Vietnam War and disarmament movements, and the current women's and gay and lesbian movements. Each has made unique contributions.

Bill Wylie Kellerman describes a public liturgical protest at an air show, during the United States bicentennial celebration, that intended to re-enact the Hiroshima bombing. The witness arose from the participants' desire to confront the demonic powers of militarism, nuclear weapon proliferation, and the national security state. "Hitler won," Kellerman insists. "His spirit rules."

> Hitler's enemies imitated him and mastered his means, which is to say, perfected them. If he could sponsor blitzkrieg, they could manage first the firebombing of Dresden and Tokyo, and then Hiroshima and Nagasaki. The bomb itself was conceived in the mind of the Nazi regime. No matter that Hitler abandoned the project. A kind of technological momentum pulled the United States version forward, not merely to production but to its use against a civilian population, and then finally to become the cornerstone of military policy. Here was sign and seal of Nazi victory.[5]

Kellerman and his colleagues fasted that day, held vigil in front of the B-29 Hiroshima-type plane (thus preventing its use in the fly-over ceremony), and crossed the rope barricade which guarded the plane to spray-paint the word DEATH on the fuselage. Ironically, only the arresting military police, he reports, saved them from serious injury at the hands of a wrathful crowd.[6]

Kellerman calls this liturgical direct action, "politically informed exorcism." The model is the public liturgy of the Catonsville Nine, among them Fathers Daniel and Philip Berrigan, who broke into a draft board office in Catonsville, Maryland, in May, 1968, and burned draft records with homemade napalm. He cites the comment of William Stringfellow:

> Politically informed exorcisms which I believe to be as exemplary as that involving the pharaoh do still occur, if occasionally. This indeed, was the witness of the Catonsville Nine, when they burned draft records in May of 1968. As those attentive to their trial . . . can apprehend, the action at Catonsville was a sacramental protest against the Vietnamese war—a liturgy of exorcism, exactly. It exposed the death idolatry of a nation which napalms children.[7]

Kellerman describes how such actions perform the function of exorcism:

> These public actions are liturgies insofar as they declare the sovereignty of God. The reign of God is celebrated and enacted in the lives of people and communities. And they are exorcisms insofar as the powers, and the power of death behind them all, are named and exposed and rebuked on behalf of human life.[8]

Kellerman and his community of peace activists have on occasion participated in fully explicit exorcisms at the headquarters and plants of weapons manufacturers using liturgies modeled specifically on the Roman Catholic rite. In keeping with the liturgy, they begin by invoking a litany of the saints, including many not traditionally mentioned, and continue with fervent prayer in the name of Christ, making the sign of the cross on sidewalks and driveways, and encircling the location with holy water.

Such public liturgies as these attest to the fact that there has emerged over recent decades the "liturgy of the social gospel" for which religious educator Wade Crawford Barclay issued a stirring call in 1926. Now being fulfilled is his fervent hope for "a vocabulary of prayer, a liturgy, that...challenges in the name of God and for the sake of humanity the selfishness and greed embodied in our economic system, and that calls upon God for the sustaining grace and inner power to resist and to overcome against all obstacles and odds."[9]

If there is reality to the spiritual realm, if institutions as powers possess an interiority, and if there is an ongoing spiritual struggle, then the struggle for peace and justice must be waged on the spiritual as well as the material front. And in this spiritual struggle the role of Christian prayer and ritual must be central.

Chapter

Healing
Prayer for
Broken
Institutions

Nothing is more rare, or more truly revolutionary, than an accurate description of reality.

Walter Wink

The church has the opportunity as perhaps never before to engage in a ministry of healing prayer for institutions, for the powers in their brokenness and fallenness. As we have seen, the institutional powers, like individuals, simultaneously are created good, fallen, and able to be redeemed. The knowledge we have of the inner life can serve us well as we seek to be instruments of God in God's redeeming, healing process of recalling the institutional powers to their God-given purposes.

A Process of Healing Prayer

But just what might it mean to lay hands upon an institution and pray for its healing? I will describe a seven-step process that many have experienced as they performed a healing ministry with particular broken institutions.

CONSTERNATION

The initial concern usually arises in an experience of consternation or puzzlement about an institution with which you have personal contact. For example, you may observe that good people are acting in destructive ways, that positive initiatives somehow get sabotaged, that genuine potential does not get realized. In one particular church just outside New York City, there was a predomi-

nant mood of hopelessness and disinterest, with astounding personal bitterness and strife among key church leaders.[1]

In another case an Illinois church had voted on whether to become
a Reconciling Congregation, that is, a congregation open to ministry
to and with all persons regardless of sexual orientation. With a number of gay and lesbian persons active and welcomed within the congregation, and with some of them in high places of leadership, there
had been good reason to be optimistic about the vote. It failed, however, causing deep consternation and disappointment.

COLLISION

The next step is to identify the fundamental impasse in the life of
the institution. One senses a collision course between the Spirit of
God and something negative at work in the congregation or other
institution. Usually the cause of the negativity lies deep in its personality. Frequently there has been a trauma or series of traumas in
the life of the institution, creating vulnerabilities into which negative
spiritual force enters. The first congregation mentioned above was
forced decades ago to leave its original site when that area was taken
by New York City to build a reservoir. The original church building
had been "drowned." It seemed that the congregation had ever since
been diverted from its mission by its collective memory of loss and
by its sense of defeat, negativism, and bitterness.

In the case of the Illinois church, the negative vote provided an
opportunity to discover the fundamental block which led to its
unloving action. What was the wound or blockage in the collective
life experience of this seemingly loving congregation that was preventing it from acting in a loving way? Spiritual discernment is
called for in such a situation.

COLLUSION

The third critical step is to acknowledge how we as healers and
activists are in collusion with the brokenness of the given institution.
Whatever is eating at the institution is likely to be preying upon our
vulnerabilities too. We may be using the tactics of the oppressor in
trying to fight the oppression, such as returning hate for hate or suc-

cumbing to its despair, resentment, and hopelessness. In the case of the New York church, the pastor was able to recognize how she too shared in the church's negative attitudes, such as its possession by the Spirit of Fear.

CONFESSION

It is then essential for us as the healers to confess and receive the forgiveness of God for our collusion with ungodly attitudes and forces. In the New York church, the pastor and those of us who had gathered to pray with her confessed how we too fall prey to hopelessness and bitterness in aspects of our lives. We then received the pronouncement of God's forgiveness and empowerment from each other. Such confession is critically important, for it diminishes the ever present danger of self-righteousness or of perpetuating unhealthy situations in which there may be a subtle payoff (for instance, providing a ready target for displaced hostility).

CONFRONTATION

We are now ready, in reliance upon the power of God, to confront the evil in the inner life of the institution that is steering it away from God's work of humanization. Many of us are well-schooled in the political care of institutions (working with its outer manifestations: electing new officers, shifting the power base, and introducing new programs). These are important and essential. But recall Wink's basic formula: $\mathbf{p}$ (powers) $\mathbf{=}$ $\mathbf{o}$ (outer manifestation) $\mathbf{+}$ $\mathbf{i}$ (inner spirituality). We are also called to address the inner spirituality of institutions and to confront the evil that besets them, using the kind of spiritual care uniquely entrusted to us as Christians. We engage in this confrontation with confidence that God really does want health and wholeness for institutions as well as for individuals and that God is already at work nudging the church or institution toward greater fidelity to its godly purpose.

CLEANSING

At this stage we enact the phrase from the prayer of Jesus, "Deliver us from evil." We courageously assume the charge Jesus gave to the disciples to "cure those who are sick, raise those who are dead, cleanse those with leprosy, *cast out demons*" (Matthew 10:8, italics added), and we do this in bold ritual form. "In the name and power of Christ," we commanded the Spirits of Fear, of Patriarchy, and of other evils, to depart from the "drowned" church.

At a church in New York State, the lay leaders were justifiably concerned about a forthcoming vote on whether the church should declare itself a Reconciling Congregation. They were not sure what was going to happen or if the timing was right. At the initiative of some laity, they went ahead of time into the room where the meeting was about to be held and prayed prayers of cleansing, asking that the space and those entering it would be freed of the Spirits of Homophobia, Fear, Arrogance, or Ignorance.

CLAIMING

After praying for cleansing, the group at that church expressly claimed the forthcoming meeting for God's yearning and prayed for God's blessing at the places where people would be sitting and speaking and making decisions. "This opened our spirits," the pastor reported, "making all of us more open to the creative work of God's Spirit; it helped us feel more serene concerning the outcome." The congregation did vote overwhelmingly to become a Reconciling Congregation, but the outcome, he testified, "was very positive indeed, on more than just that surface level."

In the case of the "drowned" church, we prayed that the old fear of the drowning waters be replaced by an embracing of the healing waters of baptism. We prayed for a renewal of baptismal vows for the members of the congregation and then went throughout the church building sprinkling it with water to claim the entire space for Christ's purposes. The pastor subsequently began to notice a significant change in key people and in the worship climate.

The Ministry of Cleansing and Claiming

The basic forms of healing prayer that are emerging in these situations are prayers of cleansing and prayers of claiming. Such prayer gives voice in specific situations to the general affirmation that all things are made in, through, and for Christ. It seeks to recall the institutional powers from what Swiss theologian Karl Barth calls their lordlessness, that is, their denial of the One who is their Lord. This recall is possible because the powers are only able to achieve, in Barth's words, "an imagined godlessness and lordlessness"; they can only act as if they were without God and without a Sovereign.

The fact that the church itself is often the focus of struggle, conflict, and brokenness should actually not surprise us. Because the church is the community especially chosen by God to name and unmask evil and to proclaim God's sovereignty, it is a prime target for evil's disruption and confusion. The struggle, however, is waged in the shadow of Christ's victory over the powers of evil, sin, and death. Joseph Weber describes the church's struggle with the demonic:

> Because the Church is the sign of Christ's victory over the demonic powers it belongs to its very nature to be under attack—usually either by direct persecution or else by subtle forces of adjustment and acculturation which wish to make the Church essentially innocuous. The world rejects the proclamation of the Church that Jesus Christ is Lord because the world is the place where the demonic powers are still trying to exercise their power. The time of the demonic powers, however, is limited. Their fight is one of desperation (Rev 2:12). The primary mission of the Church, therefore, is not just to remind the world of moral principles, or to evangelize individuals, or to assure its own institutional life. Rather, the Church is engaged in a struggle against the demonic in order to proclaim and in order to be a sign of Jesus Christ's lordship over the whole world. The Church is called by God to live in the world as if it were already fully God's renewed creation (Col 2:20-21).[2]

It should not surprise us, therefore, that many Christian activists experience the spiritual struggle with the powers most directly in church institutions themselves.

One of the most vexing issues in denominations today is the church's attitude toward its lesbian and gay members. Many of us have found ourselves caught up in the ongoing struggle against the institutionalized powers of homophobia and heterosexism. This struggle, waged at the level of my denomination's highest court, offered one of my most profound experiences of the ministry of cleansing and claiming church institutions.

The denomination's "supreme court," called the Judicial Council, was gathering to hear arguments regarding a certain woman's ordination status. She herself, as well as her partner, would be giving critical presentations to the Council in about two hours. We gathered at a time when we could be alone in the seminary chapel where the hearing would soon be held. My contribution was a prayer of cleansing, both of the space and of the minds and hearts of presenters, onlookers, and the nine Judicial Council members. The prayer was that the space and the people be cleansed of any evil power and filled with the power of God.

The woman, a church historian, contributed a litany of the saints, naming figures in church history who had stood against the power of evil in church and society and calling for them to be present with us in the strength of their historical witness. Thus we were fortified by the spiritual presence of such saints as Thelma Stevens, Georgia Harkness, Francis J. McConnell, and Michael Collins. Finally we joined in quietly singing the hymn "How Firm a Foundation." These words were never more powerful:

> "FEAR NOT, I AM WITH THEE, O BE NOT DISMAYED, FOR I AM THY GOD AND WILL STILL GIVE THEE AID;
> I'LL STRENGTHEN AND HELP THEE, AND CAUSE THEE TO STAND UPHELD BY MY RIGHTEOUS, OMNIPOTENT HAND.
> WHEN THROUGH THE DEEP WATERS I CALL THEE TO GO, THE RIVERS OF WOE SHALL NOT THEE OVERFLOW;
> FOR I WILL BE WITH THEE, THY TROUBLES TO BLESS, AND SANCTIFY TO THEE THY DEEPEST DISTRESS."

A few weeks later her partner wrote, "I truly had the sense that as the three of us prayed and witnessed, we were in heavenly company."

A Ritual for Cleansing Prayer

Create in me a clean heart, O God, and put a new and right spirit within me.   Psalm 51:10

A part of what we shared on that occasion was a cleansing prayer. The New Testament source for this is the event in Jesus' last week when he cleansed and reclaimed the temple. He ordered out the money changers as tangible representatives of the evil Spirit of Mammon, which fomented greed and exploitation in the temple institution. By word and deed Jesus reclaimed the temple from its perversion as a den of robbers for its God-given destiny as a house of prayer.

When we prayed for the cleansing of the seminary chapel where the Judicial Council was to gather, we prayed in the full awareness that wherever the United Methodist Church gathers it brings with it any uncleanness and injustice that may be in its church law. United Methodist Church law forbids the ordination and appointment of "self-avowed, practicing homosexuals," with no regard to the gifts, graces, or call from God a person may have. Its Social Principles state contradictorily that although "homosexual persons no less than heterosexual persons are individuals of sacred worth," yet "we do not condone the practice of homosexuality and consider this practice incompatible with Christian teaching."[3]

Our prayer was that this particular occasion in the life of the United Methodist Church would be cleansed of oppressive heterosexism. During the Judicial Council session and the days leading up to it, a dozen or more social action groups across the church held some form of intercessory observance, praying that heterosexism might be contained and overcome in that process. One remarkable outcome in the Judicial Council's decisions during that sitting was that the woman was reinstated and declared eligible for appointment. Another was that the Council refused to outlaw blessings of same-sex holy unions by denominational clergy, a ruling of such ramifications that the Council of Bishops issued a call for its reconsideration, a call which was rejected by the Judicial Council.[4]

When I use this ritual of cleansing, I try if at all possible to do it in the very space in which the meeting is to be held, at a time just before it is to begin, but before people have arrived for the meeting. Sometimes this can be complicated because I like to wait until building personnel have set up the room for the event so that we can pray in the room as it will be for the meeting and, if possible, move

Guidelines for a Prayer of Cleansing

1. Focus intently on the physical space, the personnel, and other outward manifestations of the institutional gathering, such as the agenda, preparatory papers, a meal which may be shared, those to whom the meeting will be reported, and so forth.

2. Include yourselves among those for whom you pray. Approach the prayer in humility and openness to God's grace and power.

3. Specifically pray for God to cleanse the following of any spirit not of God:
   a. Yourselves—your minds and hearts and bodies.
   b. The physical space of the meeting or event.
   c. Those participating in the event—one by one, if possible, and by name.
   d. The intangibles—the agenda, the worship service to take place, the leadership, the discussions, and the decisions.

4. Pray positively that God fill each of the above, (a) through (d,) with the Spirit of Christ, that Christ may be "all in all" (Ephesians 1:23).

5. Move around the room if you can (if not, do so in your imagination) and offer these prayers in specific locations and at the seats or tables of specific decision-makers.

6. If it feels right, you may also wish to sprinkle water around the room as a tangible prayer for God's cleansing, liberating power.

7. Thank God for moving among you and for God's staggering promise to reveal to the powers and authorities "the wisdom of God in its rich variety" and "to gather up all things in Christ" (Ephesians 3:10, 1:10).

8. Continue in a general intercessory stance even as the meeting or event transpires.

around to pray for decision makers at the very places they are about to occupy. I also seek to do this together with other persons who share the same concern for creating a clean heart in the life of the institution.

Where distance prevents doing such prayer at the scene of a meeting, the prayer of cleansing can still be offered. In such a case, I would urge that the group offering it engage in faith imagination, imaging in their minds and hearts the love of God sweeping away from each part of the room any ungodly power. You can image the persons to be gathered there being filled with the Holy Spirit, naming as many as possible of them. Persons at a distance can include such prayer as part of their personal prayer each day up to and including the day of the event.

A pastor decided to perform cleansing prayer before an annual meeting of the church he serves on Long Island. As he explained, the annual meeting had "for many years been afflicted by a spirit of hostility" toward the larger structure of the denomination. "So I began praying in the meeting room for peace, honesty, and an openness to God's leading," he reported, "and this year there was a palpable difference in the level of animosity. I want to do similar preparation for administrative board and trustee meetings, the worship and pastor-parish relations committee meetings—all of which need similar help. And I want to draw others into this prayerful preparation."

I urge you to find occasions to use this type of prayer as you prepare for meetings and confrontations fraught with particular tension and possibility. Ideally, gather with selected others to join you. Act upon the promise that God wants good to happen.

Ritual of Naming Lies and Declaring Truths

The power of evil is characterized as much as anything by the capacity to deceive and to misrepresent. Satan is described in the Revelation to John (12:9) as "the deceiver of the whole world." Thus we should expect that the powers of the order of domination would perpetrate an abundance of lies and falsehoods. These lies infect the church and other institutions we hold dear. They can also infect us as individuals. When such lies rise up and become stumbling blocks, there is an opportunity for the church to use its authority to unmask the lies and to declare the truth of God in the face of the lies.

A Ritual of Naming Lies and Declaring Truths can be part of our pastoral care for each other as healing activists. I was personally the recipient of such care from a mutual support group of clergy. During one of our gatherings I shared that I felt physically and emotionally debilitated and that this related to the death of my father some months before. I said that I knew that it was acceptable, even necessary, for me to take special time to grieve but that I was nevertheless hard on myself, expecting to be as productive as ever. On some deep level, I even felt I needed to be extra-productive in order to make up for what my father could no longer do in life.

In one of the most gracious acts I have experienced, my colleagues, with my permission, moved into a ritual of lies and truths, which had been developed by Tilda Norberg in her ministry of therapy and healing. The group named each lie and then declared the concomitant truth, anointing my forehead with oil as they declared in unison:

> IT IS A *LIE* THAT YOU CANNOT TAKE TIME AND ENERGY TO GRIEVE FOR YOUR FATHER.
> THE *TRUTH* IS THAT THIS IS A SPECIAL GOD-GIVEN TIME OF GRIEVING FOR YOU. . . .

And so it went, with four or five declarations. I felt truly ministered to and put on the road to wholeness in a fresh way. Since then I have become even more convinced of the power of such a Ritual of Naming Lies and Declaring Truths for our ministry, not only to one another but to institutions as well.

During a social action spirituality retreat I led in Maryland, participants surfaced their concern about persons in their church judicatory advocating for a return to patriarchal practices. This defense of a male-dominated church and world was occasioned by an ecumenical gathering of women, the now-famous Re-Imagining Conference. An Op-Ed column in the judicatory newspaper was read out loud during free time, to much shock, chagrin, and derision. It said, in part:

The real issue is patriarchy. The Old Testament, the New Testament, the early church, the Reformation, and recent church history are full of it. I fully believe in it and support it. Many women do also. "The whole of our faith is based on the concept of a godly patriarchy—beginning with God Himself. And Jesus Christ is the supreme revelation of this godly patriarchy. To the extent that this faith has been believed and practiced through the ages and around the world, it has produced orderly, peaceful, healthy, prosperous, moral societies. And to the extent that it has not been believed and practiced, life on this globe has become chaotic and degenerate.[5]

The reading of this declaration energized the retreat in a remarkable way, and as our retreat theme was addressing the principalities and powers, the focus became specifically the Spirit of Patriarchy. Small groups prepared different rituals for a closing worship service, which included a prayer of confession prepared by the men in the group; a song written by area clergywomen, beginning "Bring your battered spirit; bring your broken dreams"; and a commissioning service during which hands were laid on each in turn, as a verse was sung of "I will raise you up on eagles' wings." It was a very moving service.

It was this event that demonstrated to me how a Ritual of Naming Lies and Declaring Truths could be useful in a group facing institutional evil. I share the ritual that I created on that occasion as an example of the kind of ritual that could be adapted for a wide variety of situations:

WE DECLARE IT A LIE THAT "JESUS CHRIST IS THE SUPREME REVELATION" OF "GODLY PATRIARCHY."
THE TRUTH IS THAT JESUS REJECTED PATRIARCHAL PRIVILEGE, "EMPTIED HIMSELF, TAKING THE FORM OF A SLAVE," AND ESTABLISHED A DISCIPLESHIP OF EQUALS WITH HIS FOLLOWERS.

IT IS A LIE THAT WHEN PATRIARCHY HAS BEEN REJECTED, "LIFE ON THIS GLOBE HAS BECOME CHAOTIC AND DEGENERATED."
THE TRUTH IS THAT IT IS PATRIARCHY WHICH HAS DEMEANED WOMEN AND MEN, RATIONALIZED VIOLENCE AGAINST WOMEN, CHILDREN, AND STRANGERS, AND SUPPORTED SLAVERY.

IT IS A LIE THAT ORDER, PEACE, AND MORALITY DEPEND UPON THE PERPETUATION OF PATRIARCHAL PRIVILEGE. THE TRUTH IS THAT AS WOMEN AND MEN ARE MOVED BY THE SPIRIT OF GOD TO CHALLENGE PATRIARCHY, WE ARE GIVEN A FORETASTE OF THE REIGN OF GOD AND ITS RELATIONSHIPS OF RECIPROCITY, EQUALITY, PARTNERSHIP, AND MUTUAL RESPECT, FOR IN CHRIST "THERE IS NO LONGER MALE AND FEMALE." (GALATIANS 3:28)

We sometimes forget that every declaration of faith, from the classic creeds of the church down to present-day affirmations, implies the rejection of something else. The earliest Christian confession, "Jesus is *Kyrios*," usually rendered as Jesus is Lord or Sovereign, was a rejection of the assumed sovereignty of Caesar. To declare faith in Christ means a rejection of racism, sexism, and every other form of exploitation, as well as fear, revenge, apathy, and deceit. A Ritual of Naming Lies and Declaring Truths offers a powerful way of making the appropriate confession of faith for specific situations you may be facing.

Chapter

Exorcising the Social Demons

As you go, proclaim the good news, "The dominion of heaven has come near." Cure those who are sick, raise those who are dead, cleanse those with leprosy, cast out demons.
Matthew 10:7-8

In Jesus' day it was normal practice for money changers to sit at tables in the Jerusalem temple precincts, daily changing Roman coinage for temple coinage, while pocketing an exorbitant commission. But Jesus unmasks the evil spirit at work in this system and names it for what it is—Greed, or Mammon. He declares it unwelcome and idolatrous. He quotes scripture to the agents of this oppressive system, "My house shall be called a house of prayer for all the nations," and then levels his own charge, "but you have made it a den of robbers" (Mark 11:17). According to Mark, this precipitates his arrest and subsequent sentencing to death: "And when the chief priests and scribes heard [what Jesus had done], they kept looking for a way to kill him" (Mark 11:18).

Jesus' cleansing of the temple is a dramatized social exorcism with broad social implications. There are situations in which it is clear that institutions serve either God or the Great Deceiver, and this is one. Jesus' action confirms the appropriateness of social exorcism by those of us called to continue his ministry to the principalities and powers.

Increasingly, persons involved in Christian healing ministry are being led to employ explicit rituals of exorcism, that is, deliverance from evil spirits, with persons in special need. This evolution has not been helped by sensational treatment of deliverance, as in the film *The Exorcist*. But there are those who have reintroduced the use of healing rituals of deliverance and exorcism in pastorally responsible ways. I myself have observed personal deliverance first-hand as part of my wife's healing and counseling ministry.

Liturgically, too, there is an ongoing recovery of an understanding that Christian faith entails the rejection of evil. The baptismal covenant service in the United Methodist tradition, building on ancient church tradition, now requires adult baptismal candidates and confirmands to answer positively to the question, "Do you renounce the spiritual forces of wickedness, reject the evil powers of this world, and repent of your sin?"

In the Roman Catholic Church, the Rite of Christian Initiation of Adults, the process by which adults are prepared for baptism and church membership, makes explicit use of prayers of exorcism. A confirmation catechesis for high school students includes, among others, these prayers of exorcism:

> LORD, OUR GOD, TAKE THE SPIRIT OF SUPERFICIALITY, THE SPIRIT OF PREJUDICE, THE SPIRIT OF RACISM AND SEXISM, AND BANISH THEM FOREVER FROM THE LIVES OF THESE YOUNG PEOPLE.

> LORD, OUR GOD, TAKE THE SPIRIT OF DARKNESS AND DECEPTION, THE SPIRIT OF SELF-SERVICE AND PRIDE, AND BANISH THEM FOREVER FROM THE LIVES OF THESE YOUNG PEOPLE.[1]

Gradually such rites should introduce a deeper awareness of the Christian life as one of participation in an inner and outer struggle with God against powers not of God.

A ritual of social exorcism enacts the reality that the power of the demonic is circumscribed and that the fight of the demonic powers is one of desperation. These powers can only pretend to be autonomous, in control of their own destiny and not subject to the power of God. To their great consternation, in fact, God is able to use them to serve God's purposes. As theologian Karl Barth says, we live in a world that has already been de-demonized in Jesus Christ and one day will be fully so.

Jesus' command to cast out demons opens a whole new arena for the Christian social activist to give pastoral care, through word and deed, to the institutional powers in their brokenness and to join God in raising signs of their redemption. Some Christian activists find an explicit form of social exorcism to be an important part of their ministry of healing, embodying the ministry of cleansing and claiming in its fullest form. I would like to describe several instances of this form of social action ministry.

Social Exorcism in the Wake of Church and School Closings

Persons associated with the Catholic Worker center in inner-city Philadelphia reacted with disappointment and anger to the announcement in April 1993 that nine Roman Catholic churches and five Catholic schools in their North Philadelphia neighborhood would be closed. Repeated requests to meet with Cardinal Anthony Bevilacqua were denied.[2]

Catholic Worker leaders had been deeply sensitized to the plight of the poor. Susan Dietrich, of a well-to-do family in Manhattan Beach, California, had felt the call to develop the local Catholic Worker house in Philadelphia. Residents of the house glean their meals from food banks and their clothing from charity, and they offer food, clothing, and housing for neighbors and tutor dozens of schoolchildren. The other key leader, Frank Maimone, was converted from a life of drug abuse by reading the autobiography of Trappist monk Thomas Merton. He spent three weeks at Merton's former abbey in Kentucky, considered joining the Trappists, but then decided his call was to join the Philadelphia Catholic Worker house. Two years later he and Susan married. The four Catholic Worker residents received a glowing newspaper write-up, which described their life of voluntary communal poverty (two Worker houses ran on $20,000 a year, and much of that went for community members' basic needs) and characterized them as "a charming combination" of hippie, do-gooder, and saint. But that was before the church and school closings.

To protest the impending school closing, Frank Maimone fasted for fourteen days. His protest was fueled by the circumstances of the announcement, which came one month after Cardinal Bevilacqua proclaimed that an archdiocesan fund-raising campaign had received $101 million in pledges and collected $26 million up front. Maimone explained the Catholic Worker position in their local newsletter, which placed his article, "Money-Changers, Bean-Counters, and a Den of Thieves: The Corporate Church and Lazarus," next to a graphic of Christ throwing money changers out of the temple. Maimone contended that the archdiocese was behaving in violation of a recommendation in a 1979 pastoral letter by the United States Catholic bishops, which urgently recommended "the continuation and expansion of Catholic schools in the inner cities and other disadvantaged areas" and added that "no sacrifice can be so great, no price can be so high, no short-range goals can be so important as to warrant the lessening" of the church's commitment in minority neighborhoods.

Maimone concluded that the decision of the archdiocese was based on "sinful criteria," namely, racism and classism. "The corporate Church," he contended, "continues to prostitute itself to the highest bidder, leaving pastorals, encyclicals, and even the gospels as merely empty words." "Somewhere along the line," he said, "the church has made the decision to abandon holding corporate America to a Christian model and decided, instead, to imitate its 'success.'" He concluded, "The poor have no place in our archdiocese's image of a suburban 21st century church."

The Catholic Worker members reacted immediately to the closings by organizing the Catholic Coalition to Save Our Faith, which orchestrated weekly rallies outside the archdiocesan headquarters. The coalition, which was meeting weekly at one of the Catholic Worker houses, accused the cardinal of abandoning poor North Philadelphia Catholics. It charged the diocese with deliberately exaggerating the extent of the fiscal woes blamed for the church and school closings and requested that the church's financial records be made public.

Having met total rejection in their request for a meeting with the cardinal, Maimone and twenty others connected to the coalition organized a gathering outside archdiocesan offices at which a priest conducted the Catholic rite of exorcism in order to rid the church headquarters of a "diabolical infestation" of greed. "We do not question his [the cardinal's] faith or morals," explained Maimone. "We're questioning a corporate decision." Predictably, a spokesman for the church described the ritual as "a detestable publicity stunt." Though critics charged them with disloyalty to the church, they angrily rejected these charges. Susan and Frank, by the way, attended Catholic Mass three to five times weekly and arranged for it to be offered every Wednesday at a Catholic Worker house. The point of their protests and of the exorcism, they maintained, was to cleanse the church institution from the worship of the financial bottom line—from Mammon—and set it free to be the church.

A few days after the exorcism, Maimone and a colleague were arrested and charged with defiant trespass for entering the archdiocesan offices to request a meeting with the cardinal. The school and church closings did proceed as planned. A year later, however, subsequent archdiocesan attempts to close Catholic institutions in nearby Chester were successfully stalled, and plans for additional closings in another part of Philadelphia had been put on hold as a result of the outcry against the closings in North Philadelphia. The priest who performed the exorcism was disciplined.

Confronting the Spirit of Apartheid

My first public use of something approaching social exorcism was quite timid. In March 1985, I was the organizer of one of the daily demonstrations in front of the South African consulate in New York City involving the ritualized arrest of over one hundred United Methodists from the New York and Northern New Jersey Conferences. At a worship service prior to that witness I preached on the power of Christ over apartheid and then led the assembled group in this statement of renunciation of the power of apartheid:

WE ACT TODAY, IN THE NAME OF JESUS CHRIST, TO BREAK THE POWER OF SIN AND DEATH.
WE DECLARE THAT IN JESUS CHRIST THE POWER OF APARTHEID IS BROKEN AND IN THE FULLNESS OF TIME WILL FALL.
WE THEREFORE RENOUNCE ANY POWER THAT APARTHEID IN SOUTH AFRICA MAY HAVE OVER OUR PERSONAL LIVES, OVER THE

UNITED METHODIST CHURCH, ITS AGENCIES AND CONFERENCES, OVER OUR INVESTMENTS OR PROGRAMS, OR OVER OUR LOCAL CHURCHES AND OUR MINISTRIES WITHIN THEM.

This was a beginning, and from it would eventually flow the further development of a ritual of social exorcism.

Efforts were underway on a number of fronts to encourage the United Methodist General Board of Pensions (GBP), the repository of pension savings for United Methodist clergy and lay workers, to take an activist's role in promoting United States corporate disengagement from South Africa. The New York regional body of the denomination had sent an official delegation, of which I had been a part, to raise this issue at the pension board meeting some months earlier. We received a courteous hearing, but despite calls from many quarters, the board was intransigent.

Pension board policy stated that companies should stay in South Africa and work for change through the Sullivan Principles, a code of workplace and corporate conduct based on equal opportunity. Chief Buthalezi was often lifted up by board members as a black South African authority opposed to disinvestment. "Divest" was referred to as "that six-letter word." The board's chief executive contended in no uncertain terms that meeting our delegation's request would be illegal and imprudent in light of the "prudent man principle" for fiduciary responsibility and that we had no legitimate basis whatsoever for calling for a policy change. He contended that the board's espousal of the Sullivan Principles was actually more socially responsible than the growing ecumenical conviction, supported by South African churches, that economic sanctions and corporate withdrawal were critical to the struggle against apartheid.

About a year after the witness at the South African consulate, in July 1986, the Methodist Federation for Social Action (MFSA) sponsored a series of demonstrations at the pension board offices in Evanston, Illinois, that involved the quite unusual tactic of civil disobedience at a church office by the church's own members. Over a three-day period, thirty-seven arrests of church members were made by Evanston police who were called in by the board to clear the entrances we had blocked. This was only the most dramatic of numerous overtures for change in pension board policy, including petitions, picketing, meetings, and annual conference resolutions.

The situation, however, was at an impasse. The board stood adamant against disinvestment; the Methodist Federation for Social Action and most vocal opinion in the church was just as adamant in supporting it. This impasse created a very frustrating situation for many activists in the denomination, and I personally was experiencing a great deal of tension and sense of personal burden from the utter lack of movement. In spite of numerous statements, letters, attempts at dialogue, support from the South African churches for disinvestment, and even a well-orchestrated and widely publicized civil disobedience campaign, nothing was changing. Would it ever change? I wondered.

During this time I happened to be co-leader of a weeklong summer adult course on "Journey Inward, Journey Outward." Although I had not originally intended to do so, I found myself sharing there my deep frustration and anger over this deadlocked situation, recounting the physical effects I was experiencing from the stress, and admitting to the doubts I was having about my own leadership role in this issue.

I led a session in which I spoke about the possibilities for social exorcism, using as the example the act of renunciation and the witness at the South African consulate described above. A member of the class, one of those arrested at the consulate, Carolyn Watson, responded by suggesting that we, then and there, hold a deliverance service in relation to the chains which seemed to link our church and the Board of Pensions with apartheid. She prepared a liturgy for this purpose patterned after one often used with individuals. This tiny group of seven people decided to proceed with this service of social exorcism, with its focus on what we believed to be collusion between the United Methodist General Board of Pensions and the power of apartheid.

At the beginning of the social exorcism service we took some time to discern, through silence and sharing, what were the ungodly spirits that blocked the pension board as an institution from taking an aggressive, activist role in combating apartheid in South Africa despite the overwhelming sentiment in the church for it to do so. We concluded that the spirits not of God that needed to be addressed were the Spirits of Fear and Intimidation, Arrogance and

Lust for Power, Mammon, and Patriarchy. The service was a very powerful and exhausting one, embracing several hours. An indication of the degree of intensity was that two persons felt it necessary to leave in the middle of the words of exorcism, and they never returned for the final day of the class.

I personally was deeply grateful for my colleague's bold initiative to create and offer the social exorcism ritual and for the powerful experience we shared. I knew that something in me had changed; I was eager to see what difference there might be in the pension board and looked forward to the board's fall meeting in Louisville. Further, I began to entertain the idea that some of us hold a public service of social exorcism at that forthcoming meeting.

Then, just a couple of weeks later, came a big surprise: the chief executive of the pension board, widely perceived to be the strongest factor in the board's resisting the ecumenical strategy, announced, totally unexpectedly, that he would resign by year's end. This announcement had extraordinary impact upon the small group of us who had performed this social exorcism. Were we to interpret the executive's resignation as a tangible sign of God's power over the powers we had addressed in our service? Indeed, the way was opened now for new possibilities under a new executive.

I would not claim any simple cause-effect relationship, but I do believe there was some connection between our service of social exorcism and that resignation and subsequent events. This connection may not be deduced through ordinary cause-effect analysis, but in terms of the "logic" of the Spirit and her movement among us, I believe there was a powerful relationship.

Some three months later a delegation of us from MFSA gathered in Louisville to attempt again to persuade the pension board to support disinvestment. The board's Committee on Corporate and Fiduciary Responsibility had come to allow, even expect, several of us to speak with them about investments in South Africa. Six of us who had come to observe and petition met ahead of time to pray very intentionally that God would fill that meeting room in the historic Seelbach Hotel with the light of Christ's power, and would bless the public service of social exorcism that twenty-five of us planned to hold in front of the hotel the next day.

Again there was an awesome surprise waiting. The three of us who spoke discovered in making our presentation that the committee had a heretofore unknown openness toward us. The very perceptible change in the attitude with which we were received was evident, above all, by the fact that for the first time we were asked questions following our brief presentations. It was a subtle but very real change, causing those of us there to share with one another our wonderment at the palpable sense of the Spirit's presence and movement.

The next afternoon, as the cold November wind whipped about us and nearly stole our voices, some two dozen of us held a public liturgy of social exorcism in front of the Seelbach Hotel. The liturgy was based on the one we had used in July, somewhat amplified and formalized.

No members or staff of the board were present, and I do not know how much they were aware of our liturgy. An account was carried in the Louisville papers, so I am sure some were aware. But somehow it did not seem to matter whether or not they knew; our battle was not with them as individuals but with spirits that were present in the institution.

The remainder of that meeting brought some additional breakthroughs: an intense, late-night dialogue between thirty of us and about one-third of the board's members; an opportunity during the board's plenary session for me to present MFSA's dissenting view on a policy paper they were about to adopt which simply reiterated their position; and the board's decision to implement my proposal for them to hold regional meetings on the South Africa question.

In the following months, a new, open-minded chief executive was selected to head the pension board; vigorous dissent to board policy was expressed at most of the ten regional meetings; and Leon Sullivan himself replaced the Sullivan Principles with a call for corporate withdrawal. At its 1987 meetings the pension board progressively moved to an official position of urging corporate withdrawal and adopted a timetable for a selective divestment of some leading United States firms in South Africa, particularly oil companies selling to the police and military (which all oil companies in South Africa were required by law to do). While not yet meeting all our expectations, a majority on the board came to embrace a level of shareholder activism for justice which clearly represented a new direction.

Those of us agitating for change experienced a conversion as well. Our image of the pension board gradually changed from that of a faceless bureaucracy into a community of women and men who were struggling to be responsible trustees, offering to the church great sacrifices of time and energy. We who regularly attended their meetings came to love and care and pray for them. We also came to see that uniting fiduciary and social responsibility was a challenging task, one that they had not understood as central to their task when they became board members; and we were moved by the struggles and growth through which the Spirit was leading them.

I discovered that I too was caught up in the Spirit of Fear and Arrogance, and in the process of the institution's liberation I experienced liberation as well. At one critical point I realized that I was "falling in love" with the board, and the social transformation question framed itself as, How do we love this board into change? To live with that question was itself a form of liberation, a newfound Christian freedom. This whole experience demonstrated to me very strongly the special call we have to employ our spiritual gifts as part of our witness to God's socially transforming love and power.

The social exorcism service has also been used in situations as varied as challenging sexism in a Roman Catholic parish and diocese, confronting the denial of ordination to women in a Mennonite Church conference, and addressing havoc-causing sprits in divided and hurting local churches of several denominations. A group of activists in Minneapolis held a monthly social exorcism ritual, focusing not only on alien spirits in institutions, but also very specifically on those spirits within themselves which interfered with their own life and ministry.

Chapter

Performing a Ritual of Social Exorcism

The occasion for a social exorcism needs to be carefully chosen. Above all, there should be a shared context of ministry and social witness. Because this is an unusual ritual, some people may need time for orientation to the ritual and its presuppositions. It needs to be emphasized that this liturgy is genuine, and not a form of guerrilla theater or show. There should be plenty of time allotted for the service since most services, at least those in private settings, take from two and one-half to four hours. It works well to provide for a common meal following the service.

A. INITIAL SHARING

The initial period is usually a time of sharing what has been happening in people's lives around the issue of concern. Everyone needs to be brought up-to-date on recent history. Some supportive outsiders who need to be oriented may be present.

For example, when seven Mennonite women and two male sympathizers gathered to support women's ordination, sharing was intense and took over an hour. Various ones present shared what they knew of the current situation regarding women's standing in the judicatory. Of great concern was a draft statement by the board of bishops on "The Role of Christian Men as Spiritual Leaders." The statement, being considered again at a meeting that weekend, declared, "Role definitions between men and women are becoming increasingly confused." It went on to affirm what it called "the Biblical principles and guidelines that define the relationship of men to women especially as they relate to men as spiritual leaders." Acknowledging that "all believers are equal in the image of God," it raised the caveat, "this equality does not imply uniformity and the eradication of distinct roles." The clinching statement was this: "Man's leadership role was part of God's plan from creation and not simply the result of sin."

A passionate letter was shared from one congregation protesting the form and content of the statement and contending that reserving spiritual leadership for men is not biblical—"both from biblical example and from our current experience in the church." The coordinator for the social exorcism then asked how each person was feeling: empowered, oppressed, or whatever. One reported feeling burned out, wounded, lacking in energy, and unsupported in her work on behalf of women. In preparation for the social exorcism she said that she had found special meaning in the river mentioned in Psalm 46, "whose streams make glad the city of God." She felt confidence in the river of God's activity; its unstoppable flow would "make glad" regardless of her weariness and woundedness. Another shared that she had been in such a tearful place during the week that she had thought she would be a block to the group. She had contacted the convenor, who told her that, to the contrary, her honesty and tears would serve the entire group.

A woman who had been proposed for ordination but then told the judicatory did not ordain women confessed her anger at her bishop. Tearfully she recounted her struggle to get beyond her anger and said she had begun to feel some love for him. She felt she was moving toward leaving the issue in God's hands. Another woman spoke of a reference in one of Walter Wink's books to the indispensable moral role played by Civil Rights movement activists in Selma, Alabama in exposing the evil of institutionalized racism. She saw a distinct parallel in the responsibility of those gathered there to expose the evil of patriarchy.

B. INTRODUCTION AND INVOCATION

An introduction needs to be given about the service, stressing its serious intent and emphasizing that the central focus is not on the power of evil but upon the power of God in Jesus Christ over all things. The names of the powers are indeed unmasked, yet the central attention is upon Christ who is "above every name that is named" (Ephesians 1:21). In an informal setting, questions may be entertained and clarifications made. A prayer of invocation may then be offered.

C. SCRIPTURE

Excellent scripture passages to read (or better, share from memory) include Jesus' cleansing of the temple (Mark 11:15-19), Paul's declaration that "[nothing] will be able to separate us from the love of God in Christ Jesus" (Romans 8:35-39), and the declaration that all things were created in Christ, through Christ, and for Christ (Colossians 1:11-17). One should be open to additional scripture sharing by the gathered community, as time permits.

D. DISCERNMENT OF THE SPIRITS

Then time needs to be taken to discern together the spirits undermining God's intention in the situation. This can begin with a period of silence for reflection, followed by a listing of the spirits which have come to mind, and concluding with a common sensing of the key ones to name in the ritual. If the service involves a large group, this discernment should perhaps be done in advance by a smaller group.

Such discernment actually performs the function of unmasking the power of evil and should be treated as a very solemn, God-given, and even risky undertaking. The Mennonite women named the Spirits of Deceit, Fear, Domination, Arrogance, and Hatred of Women as key powers blocking the ordination of women. A social exorcism just before the outbreak of the Gulf War focused on the Spirits of Militarism, Violence, and False Patriotism. The Spirits of Domination, Contempt, and Fear are among those identified in most of these discernments.

E. CONFESSION

This phase, confession, is critical. At this time participants search their hearts for how they have in some way been complicit with the

spirits named. It is good for this confession to be spoken aloud, so
that the experience of confession and absolution is a shared one.
This helps guard against any self-righteousness, arrogance, or "we
versus they" mentality which could arise. We should not shrink from
naming social sin at work, but we do so as sinners ourselves.
Following the confession, a clear and compelling absolution is then
pronounced in the name and power of Jesus Christ. The Mennonite
women, for instance, confessed their own participation in the Spirit
of Fear (fear of rejection, fear of change, fear of confrontation, and
fear of responsibility), their failure to give support to those challenging the system, their "childhood tapes" urging acceptance of
men's domination, and their own self-righteousness.

F. HOLY COMMUNION

Then follows a sharing of Holy Communion, with the prayer of
consecration emphasizing the appropriate theme of Christ triumphant over the powers of sin and death. For instance, where a
Communion liturgy speaks of God's delivering us from slavery to sin
and death, one could also add a reference to God's deliverance from
principalities, powers, and authorities that work against God's will.
One could also pray for God "to protect us from evil and to show
forth the loving power of Christ over all things."

G. WORDS OF DELIVERANCE

First we bind these spirits from doing further evil in the institution and declare that their ties to the institution are, in the name and
power of Jesus Christ, broken:

> WE DISCERN THAT THERE ARE INFLUENCES AND SPIRITS NOT OF
> GOD WHICH ARE PREYING UPON *[NAME OF THE INSTITUTION,
> GOVERNMENT, OR ENTITY]* AND HOLDING IT CAPTIVE TO ALIEN
> PRINCIPALITIES AND POWERS.

> IN THE NAME AND POWER OF JESUS CHRIST WE BIND THESE
> SPIRITS AND POWERS NOT OF GOD SO THEY CAN DO NO MORE
> EVIL. RECEIVING GOD'S FORGIVENESS, AND WITH CONFIDENCE

> IN CHRIST, WHO CAST OUT DEMONS AND DROVE THE AGENTS OF
> MAMMON FROM THE TEMPLE, WE DECLARE THESE SPIRITS ARE
> EXPOSED, DISCREDITED, AND STRIPPED OF THEIR POWER.

> IN THE NAME AND POWER OF JESUS CHRIST WE DECLARE THAT
> ALL TIES HAVE BEEN SEVERED BETWEEN *[THE INSTITUTION]* AND
> ANY PREVIOUS INCIDENTS, INFLUENCES, HISTORY, POLICY, TRA-
> DITIONS, THEORIES, CUSTOMS, AUTHORITIES, FINANCIAL OR
> POLITICAL GROUPS, GOVERNMENT INSTITUTIONS OR INDIVIDUALS
> WHO HAVE BECOME CONDUITS, ADVISORS, OR CHANNELS MISDI-
> RECTING IT OR PERSONS WHO ARE CONNECTED TO IT, FOR
> UNGODLY ENDS.

Then we speak the words of deliverance to the Spirits of Evil:

> SPIRIT OF *[FEAR, FOR EXAMPLE]*, IN THE NAME AND POWER OF
> JESUS CHRIST, WE ORDER YOU TO DEPART FROM *[THE INSTITU-
> TION]* AND SURRENDER BEFORE GOD.

This is done for each of the spirits earlier discerned and can be repeated one or more times until those present sense that the spirit has been sufficiently addressed.

H. PRAYERS FOR RENEWAL

Then follows prayer for the renewal of the institution's purpose. For instance:

> GOD, WE THANK YOU FOR YOUR POWER OVER SPIRITS WHICH
> DEFY YOU. WE ASK YOU NOW TO CREATE IN *[THE INSTITUTION]* A
> CLEAN HEART.
> WHERE THERE WAS THE SPIRIT OF *[FEAR]* REPLACE IT WITH THE
> SPIRIT OF *[LOVE]*.
> WHERE THERE WAS THE SPIRIT OF *[PATRIARCHY]*, FILL IT WITH
> THE SPIRIT OF *[MUTUALITY]*.

Other such couplets could be Domination-Humility, Greed-Generosity, Arrogance-Humility. These can also be repeated as felt necessary.

At this point you may wish to pray for the renewal of your baptismal vows and those of any Christian decision makers involved in the given institution. This is especially appropriate in light of the recent revival of emphasis on baptism as a rejection of the power of evil. The prayer could take this form:

GOD, WE PRAY THAT CHRISTIAN DECISION MAKERS, AND WE OURSELVES, MAY BE STRENGTHENED IN OUR RESOLVE TO RENOUNCE THE SPIRITUAL FORCES OF WICKEDNESS, TO REJECT THE EVIL POWERS OF THIS WORLD, AND TO REPENT OF OUR SIN. ENABLE US TO ACCEPT THE FREEDOM AND POWER YOU GIVE US TO RESIST EVIL, INJUSTICE, AND OPPRESSION IN WHATEVER FORMS THEY PRESENT THEMSELVES AND TO BE FAITHFUL TO THE INBREAKING OF YOUR REIGN.

This closing prayer might well include the actual names of the participants and of the decision makers of the institution. At the ritual held during the meeting of the denominational pension board, the names of the staff and board members were spoken. The service during the meeting of a denomination's top judicial body included the names of its nine members.

J. PRAYERS OF THANKSGIVING AND FOR CONTINUING WITNESS FOR JUSTICE

The prayer of thanksgiving is a time to thank God for God's present and continuing action to overcome evil and to ask for strength for the continuing witness for justice. The prayers could embrace both the particular context for this service as well as situations in which others are working for justice.

K. EXHORTATION AND BENEDICTION

A closing exhortation in the words of Ephesians 6:10-18 is very appropriate: "Finally, be strong in Christ and in the strength of Christ's power. Put on then the whole armor of God. . . ."

At the end of the reading, one could help participants to accept this empowerment and protection in a deeply personal way by having them repeat after the leader a Litany of Confirmation based upon the passage. It could go something like this:

> I TAKE UPON MYSELF THE WHOLE ARMOR AND PROTECTION OF GOD.
> I FASTEN THE BELT OF TRUTH AROUND MY WAIST.
> I PUT ON THE BREASTPLATE OF RIGHTEOUSNESS.
> ON MY FEET I PLACE THAT WHICH MAKES ME READY TO PROCLAIM THE GOSPEL OF PEACE.
> I TAKE UP THE SHIELD OF FAITH TO QUENCH ALL THE FLAMING ARROWS OF THE EVIL ONE.
> I PUT ON THE HELMET OF SALVATION AND THE SWORD OF THE SPIRIT, WHICH IS THE WORD OF GOD.
> I WILL PRAY IN THE SPIRIT AT ALL TIMES, KEEP ALERT, AND PER-SEVERE IN SUPPLICATION FOR ALL THE SAINTS.

A benediction such as this concludes the ritual:

> NOW TO THE ONE WHO BY THE POWER AT WORK WITHIN US IS ABLE TO ACCOMPLISH ABUNDANTLY FAR MORE THAN WE CAN ASK OR IMAGINE, TO GOD BE GLORY IN THE CHURCH AND IN CHRIST JESUS TO ALL GENERATIONS, FOREVER AND EVER. AMEN. (EPHESIANS 3:20-21)

Participants are likely to feel exhausted at the close of the ritual, not only because it may have taken several hours, but also because they have been struggling with very real principalities and powers. A time of relaxing and breaking bread together will feel very appropriate.

A Concluding Example

One afternoon a small group of persons gathered with Sister Catherine, at her request, for social exorcism prayer. She was feeling an enormous burden in the Roman Catholic Church's exclusion of women from ordained ministry. A member of a parish ministry team, she was filled with anger at the priests she worked with, though she felt uncomfortable about having such feelings. "There were times I was so angry," she said, "that I couldn't go to mass because of my anger at the priests for being the enfleshment of the sexist oppression in the church." Over many years she had led Catholic catechu-

mens through the Rite of Christian Initiation of Adults, including
the prayers of exorcism. She had seen powerful transformations in
persons dealing with their oppressions and hoped that God would
work through the social exorcism prayer to address her oppression
by the church.

Going into the ritual she was anxious. "I was scared," she recalled.

> I felt that I was turning a corner by saying out loud, sort of pub-
> licly, what I had been feeling—that there was something really
> wrong in the church, not something I needed to adjust myself
> to, but to which the church needed to adjust. Liturgy is very
> important to me and to say liturgically that the church was
> involved in evil was a very important step for me.

It was important to her, she said, that men, including a Catholic
priest, were present in the group she called together and that both
an unordained and an ordained woman were present. She also wanted the group to be ecumenical because it had been in an ecumenical
clergy group that she "first really felt equal in ministry."

When asked what difference the ritual of social exorcism had
meant to her, she replied:

> It was a really powerful experience. Something you can't
> explain happens; there's another Power at work. I didn't expe-
> rience any immediate change, but it kicked the wheel in the
> right direction. A month or so afterwards, I was able to begin
> to let go of my anger at the priests, and began to feel compas-
> sion for them. My resentment shifted to the system, a system
> by which they were restricted and confined just as I was. That
> anger gradually went away, and I feel relief came from the
> prayer we did.

Through the social exorcism liturgy she also found empowerment
in her ministry:

> The experience turned out to be very empowering for my sense
> of ministry. I had been feeling a power over me that was saying

A Ritual of Social Exorcism

Invocation and Introduction

Scripture *[Mark 11:15-19, Romans 8:35-39, Colossians 1:11-17, or other pertinent passages may be used.]*

Discernment of the Spirits and Powers *[Following a period of silent prayer for discernment, the gathered community identifies the spirits not of God which hold captive the given institution; for instance, these may be the Spirits of Mammon, Domination, Fear, Greed, Arrogance, or Contempt for the Poor.]*

Confession *[It is critical for participants to search their hearts for ways in which they collaborate with the spirits and powers named.]*

Absolution

Holy Communion *[This emphasizes Christ triumphant over the powers of sin and death.]*

Words of Deliverance

We discern that there are influences and spirits not of God which are preying upon *[name of the institution, government, or entity]* and holding it captive to alien principalities and powers.

In the name and power of Jesus Christ, we bind these spirits and powers not of God so they can do no more evil.

Receiving God's forgiveness, and with confidence in Christ, who cast out demons and drove the agents of Mammon from the temple, we declare these spirits are exposed, discredited, and stripped of their power.

In the name and power of Jesus Christ we declare that all ties have been severed between *[the institution]* and any previous incidents; influences; history; policy; traditions; theories; customs; authorities; financial or political groups; and government institutions or individuals who have become conduits, advisors, or channels misdirecting it, or persons who are connected to it, for ungodly ends.

Let us now order the ungodly spirits to depart.

   Spirit of *[insert name]*, in the name and power of Jesus Christ we order you to depart from *[the institution]* and surrender before God.

   Spirit of *[insert name]*, in the name and power of Jesus Christ we order you to depart from *[the institution]* and surrender before God.
   [Continue for each spirit, and repeat as you feel led.]

Prayer for Renewal of the Institution's Purpose

   O God, we thank you for your power over spirits that defy you. We ask you now to fill *[the institution]* with a clean heart.

   Where there was _____, fill it with _____.
   Where there was _____, fill it with _____.

[Continue with each spirit named above. Examples of couplets in the above prayer would be Domination-Humility, Greed-Generosity, Arrogance-Humility, Contempt for the Poor-Solidarity with the Poor.]

[You may at this point also wish to pray for the renewal of the baptismal vows of any known Christian leaders of the given institution.]

Prayer of Thanksgiving and for the Continuing Witness for Justice

Exhortation *[Ephesians 6:10-18 is especially appropriate here.]*

Benediction

I didn't have anything to give anymore. I was doubting myself, thinking, "How could I have ever thought I had something to give?" I can definitely say that this power was broken in our liturgy. It enabled me to think about new possibilities for ministry for me in my church, even though there seemed to be no practical way to realize them. I found myself letting go of things binding me, including the sense that there were things I couldn't do because I was a woman and not ordained.

Finally, she related how she has experienced new opportunities opening up and changed behavior on the part of "the system":

Every time I've taken initiative and expected resistance, I've found affirmation instead. I sensed the powers loosening their hold on us and loosening their hold on the structures. This has had an effect on the priests—perhaps because I'm different. I notice the pastor taking some chances he shouldn't be taking— as in allowing me to do the homily (though not calling it a homily!). Some movement has been possible within the constraints; the system has found a way to act differently.

Sister Catherine's moving account speaks for itself. I hope her story and those of others serve to introduce you to some new ways to unite prayer and social action.

Epilogue

Claiming All Things for God

I hope these pages suggest to you some ways to forge a stronger unity between prayer and action as you seek to pave the way for institutions to more fully serve the intention for which they were conceived in Christ. In particular my prayer is

1. that we claim our personal being for God and that we practice and enjoy, whether in action or in retreat, the "sacrament of the present moment";

2. that we claim our meetings as belonging to God, allowing them to be theaters of discernment of God's gracious intention for us; and

3. that in prayer and in social action we claim for God the life of institutions—churches, police departments, schools, criminal justice systems, Congress, or whatever—rejecting all that stands in the way of God's redemptive power.

I have recommended forms of spiritual practice that in my experience have enabled socially concerned Christians to focus their intentionality. I believe they can be helpful in filling the void that exists between our spirituality and our witness for social transformation. But we should never make any spiritual practice the object of devotion. What finally matters is the intention we bring; the particular practice is only the means for expressing the intention.

I am also aware that there are many forms of spiritual practice and that my particular preferences may not be those of all others. While I passionately hope you will try the forms of spiritual practice I have suggested, my deeper hope is that my passion to bring intentional spiritual practice together with action for justice will fan the flame of your passion to do the same as you feel led by the Spirit.

As you increasingly become a contemplative-in-action, I anticipate you will experience increasing courage, boldness, creativity, enthusiasm, joy, confidence, humility, and intentionality. Let the divine energy and wisdom flow through us—that God's hidden presence in all things may be visible, and that the fullness of God's Reign may be manifest.

Notes

1. Spiritual Practice and Social Action

1. Tilden H. Edwards, *Living with Apocalypse: Spiritual Resources for Social Compassion* (San Francisco: Harper & Row, 1984), 5.
2. See Taylor Branch, *Parting the Waters: America in the King Years 1954-63* (New York: Simon and Schuster, 1988), 12.
3. Gerhard Wehr, "German Spirituality," in *The Westminster Dictionary of Christian Spirituality*, ed. Gordon S. Wakefield (Philadelphia: Westminster Press, 1983), 172.
4. Sidney H. Evens, "Anglican Spirituality," in *The Westminster Dictionary*, 16.
5. Gerald G. May, *Pilgrimage Home: The Conduct of Contemplative Practice in Groups* (New York: Paulist Press, 1979), 7.

2. Guilt and Grace

1. Laurence A. Wagley, "Prayer for the Hurried, the Undisciplined and the Disorganized," *The Christian Century* 110, no. 10 (1993): 323.
2. Ibid.
3. Gerald May, "Gentleness," *Praying* (November-December 1993): 8-10.
4. The following exercise is inspired by "Basic Contemplative Exercise" in Gerald G. May, *The Awakened Heart: Living Beyond Addiction* (San Francisco: Harper & Row, 1991), 115-18.
5. See Exodus 33:3 and Acts 7:51.
6. E.E. Cummings, "i thank You God for most this amazing," in *E.E. Cummings: Complete Poems, 1913-1962* (New York: Harcourt Brace Jovanovich, 1972), 663.
7. Thomas R. Kelly, *A Testament of Devotion* (New York: Harper & Bros., 1941), 108-9, 111.
8. Ibid.
9. Ibid.
10. Ibid., italics added.

3. The Silent Tyranny of the Modern Worldview

1. John Horgan, "Anti-omniscience: An Eclectic Gang of Thinkers Pushes at

Knowledge's Limits," *Scientific American* (August 1994): 20-22.

2. Ibid.
3. Walter Wink, *Engaging the Powers: Discernment and Resistance in a World of Domination* (Philadelphia: Fortress Press, 1992), 5.
4. Walter Wink, *Unmasking the Powers: The Invisible Forces That Determine Human Existence* (Philadelphia: Fortress Press, 1986), 2.
5. Wink, *Engaging the Powers*, 5.
6. Gregory Baum, *Theology and Society* (New York: Paulist Press, 1987), 129.
7. Ibid.
8. Sandra Schneiders, *The Revelatory Text: Interpreting the New Testament as Sacred Scripture* (San Francisco: HarperCollins, 1991), 21.
9. Baum, *Theology and Society*, 134.
10. Gregory Baum, *Religion and Alienation: A Theological Reading of Sociology* (New York: Paulist Press, 1975), 185.
11. Wink, *Engaging the Powers*, 7.

4. Tool of Domination or Wellspring of Resistance?

1. Gregory Baum, *Theology and Society* (New York: Paulist Press, 1987), 292.
2. Harry Magdoff and Paul M. Sweezy, "Marxism and Religion" in *Churches in Struggle: Liberation Theologies and Social Change in North America*, ed. William K. Tabb (New York: Monthly Review Press, 1986), 195.
3. Paul Tillich, *Political Expectation* (New York: Harper & Row, 1971), 110.
4. *Selections from the Prison Notebooks of Antonio Gramsci*, ed. and trans. by Quintin Hoare and Geoffrey Norwell Smith (New York: International Publishers, 1971), 163.
5. Ibid., 80, n. 49.
6. For further details on the Ward file, see George D. McClain, "Social Ministry and Surveillance: Harry F. Ward and the Federal Bureau of Investigation," in *Rethinking Methodist History: A Bicentennial Historical Consultation*, ed. Russell E. Richey and Kenneth E. Rowe (Nashville: Kingswood Books, 1985), 212-19.
7. See Gil Dawes, "Working People and the Church: Profile of a Liberated Church in Reactionary Territory" in *Churches in Struggle*, ed. Tabb, 223-39.
8. James G. Waters, *New York Times*, 20 August 1994, 9.
9. John Kavanaugh, *Following Christ in a Consumer Society: The Spirituality of Cultural Resistance*, rev. ed. (Maryknoll, N.Y.: Orbis Books, 1991), 9.
10. Ibid., 12.
11. Michael H. Crosby, *Thy Will Be Done: Praying the Our Father as a Subversive Activity* (Maryknoll, N.Y.: Orbis Books, 1977), 2.
12. Ibid., 3.

5. The Crisis in Biblical Authority

1. Sandra Schneiders, *The Revelatory Text: Interpreting the New Testament as Sacred Scripture* (San Francisco: HarperCollins, 1991), 3.

2. Ibid., 20.
3. John Ball, "Sermon to the People," quoted in *A Radical Reader: The Struggle for Change in England, 1381-1914*, ed. Christopher Hampton (Norwich: Penguin Books, 1984), 51.
4. Schneiders, *The Revelatory Text*, 20.
5. Itumeleng J. Mosala, *Biblical Hermeneutics and Black Theology in South Africa* (Grand Rapids: William B. Eerdmans, 1989), 121.
6. Norman K. Gottwald, *The Hebrew Bible in Its Social World and in Ours* (Atlanta: Scholars Press, 1993), 363.

6. Recovering the Psalms as the Voice of Protest

1. *The New Oxford Annotated Bible with the Apocryphal/Deuterocanonical Books*, New Revised Standard Version, ed. Bruce M. Metzger and Roland E. Murphy (New York: Oxford Universtiy Press, 1991), 710.
2. Norman K. Gottwald, *The Hebrew Bible—A Socio-Literary Introduction* (Philadelphia: Fortress Press, 1985), 602.
3. Ibid., 285-86.
4. Ibid., 539.
5. Psalm 35:1-2, 17, 22-23, 25, 27-28; personal pronouns have been made plural.

7. The Risk of Faithful Surrender

1. Gerald G. May, *Will and Spirit: A Contemplative Psychology* (San Francisco: Harper & Row, 1982), 1-3, 6.
2. Quoted in Corita Clarke, *A Spirituality for Active Ministry* (Kansas City: Sheed and Ward, 1991), 47.
3. Tilden H. Edwards, *Spiritual Friend: Reclaiming the Gift of Spiritual Direction* (New York: Paulist Press, 1980), 17-18.
4. Thomas Keating, *Intimacy with God* (New York: Crossroad, 1994), 64. For a detailed description, see his influential book, *Open Mind, Open Heart: The Contemplative Dimension of the Gospel* (Amity, N.Y.: Amity House, 1986).
5. Douglas V. Steere, *Dimensions of Prayer* (New York: Women's Division, Board of Global Ministries, The United Methodist Church, 1962), 95.
6. Henri Nouwen, *The Way of the Heart* (New York: Seabury Press, 1981), 33-34.
7. W. Paul Jones, *Trumpet at Full Moon: An Introduction to Christian Spirituality as Diverse Practice* (Louisville: Westminster/John Knox Press, 1992).
8. Steere, *Dimensions of Prayer*, 106.
9. See Constance Fitzgerald, O.C.D., "Impasse and Dark Night," in *Living with Apocalypse: Spiritual Resources for Social Compassion*, ed. Tilden H. Edwards (San Francisco: Harper & Row, 1984), 105.
10. Edwin H. Friedman, *Generation to Generation: Family Process in Church and Synagogue* (New York: The Guilford Press, 1985), 42.

8. Discerning the Yearning of God

1. Lanny Wolfe, "Surely the Presence of the Lord" (Cleveland, Tenn.: Pathway Press, 1977).
2. Most of these assumptions are drawn from Tilda Norberg and Robert D. Webber, *Stretch Out Your Hand: Exploring Healing Prayer* (Cleveland: United Church Press, 1990), 97-99.
3. Article 97 #2 of *General Constitutions of the Order of Franciscans Minor*, quoted by Hermann Schaluck in "New Ways of Thinking," *Pax et Bonum* (3 September 1994): 4.
4. Norberg and Webber, *Stretch Out Your Hand*, 98-99.
5. Use of a common breath prayer is the recommendation of Larry Peacock in "Prayer: Like Yeast in Bread," *Raising Prayer to a Lifestyle* (October-December 1993): 2.
6. In a fine study which I encountered when this manuscript was complete, Charles M. Olsen reports finding "a high level of frustration and even disillusionment among laypeople with their experience on church boards, much of it due to a lack of a 'missing element'—spirituality" (p. xi). He shares the successful experience of a number of church boards in transforming the agendas of meetings and developing a new paradigm of "meeting as worship." Olsen offers some excellent concrete suggestions for creative ways to pray in meetings and for the weaving of personal, organizational, and biblical stories. See Charles M. Olsen, *Transforming Church Meetings into Communities of Spiritual Leaders* (Bethesda: The Alban Institute, 1995).
7. Danny E. Morris, *Yearning to Know God's Will: A Workbook for Discerning God's Guidance for Your Life* (Grand Rapids: Zondervan, 1991), 42-46.
8. I have given the name Prayer-Action Cycle to this process. Sister Miriam Cleary and her associates at The Center for Spirituality and Justice, Bronx, New York, who developed the form that I first encountered, call it the Experience Cycle. For more information on their spiritual direction program, contact them at 39 Willow Drive, New Rochelle, NY 10805.
9. Joe Holland and Peter Henriot have elaborated on this phase in a helpful way in their book, *Social Analysis* (Washington, D.C.: Center of Concern, 1983).

9. Spiritual Struggle with the Powers

1. See Walter Wink: *Naming the Powers* (Philadelphia: Fortress Press, 1984), *Unmasking the Powers: The Invisible Forces That Determine Human Existence* (Philadelphia: Fortress Press, 1986), and *Engaging the Powers: Discernment and Resistance in a World of Domination* (Philadelphia: Fortress Press, 1992).
2. Bill Wylie Kellerman, "Spiritual Warfare and Economic Justice," *Witness* (May 1994): 16.
3. James Brooke, "In These Grim Jails, All Hope Is Easily Abandoned," *New York Times*, 19 October 1994. All the data that follow about Venezuelan prisons were supplied by this article.

4. Ibid.
5. Ibid.
6. Wink, *Engaging the Powers*, 65. The quotes from Wink that follow are also from this book. Page numbers are given in the text.
7. Sara Rimer, "In a Bitter Campaign Season, a Candidate Rejects the Politics of Cynicism," *New York Times*, 17 October 1994.

10. Liberating Christian Ritual for Social Transformation

1. Richard Rohr, "Prayer as Political Activity," *Praying* (July-August 1989): 12.
2. See Elizabeth Schüssler-Fiorenza, *In Memory of Her: A Feminist Theological Reconstruction of Christian Origins* (New York: Crossroad, 1983).
3. Walter Wink, *Engaging the Powers: Discernment and Resistance in a World of Domination* (Philadelphia: Fortress, 1992), 93, 353-54.
4. See Paul L. Lehmann, *Ethics in a Christian Context* (New York: Harper & Row, 1963), 101: "The Christian *koinonia* is the foretaste and the sign in the world that God has always been and is contemporaneously doing what it takes to make and to keep human life human. This is the will of God 'as it was in the beginning, is now, and ever shall be, world without end.'"
5. Kellerman, *Seasons of Faith and Conscience: Kairos, Confession, and Liturgy* (Maryknoll, N.Y.: Orbis, 1991), 89.
6. Ibid., 62.
7. Quoted by Kellerman in *Seasons*, 103, from William Stringfellow, *An Ethic for Christians and Other Aliens in a Strange Land* (Waco: Word Books, 1973), 150.
8. Kellerman, *Seasons*, 105.
9. Wade Crawford Barclay, *Challenge and Power: Meditations and Prayers in Personal and Social Religion* (Nashville: Abingdon-Cokesbury Press, 1936), 13.

11. Healing Prayer for Broken Institutions

1. The story of this church comes from Norberg and Webber, *Stretch Out Your Hand: Exploring Healing Prayer* (Cleveland: United Church Press, 1990), 70-74.
2. Joseph Weber, "Christ's Victory Over the Powers," in *Above Every Name: The Lordship of Christ and Social Systems*, ed. Thomas E. Clarke (Ramsey, N.J.: Paulist Press, 1980), 75.
3. *The Book of Discipline of The United Methodist Church* (Nashville: The United Methodist Publishing House, 1996), 89.
4. Alas, the denomination's highest legislative body did vote in 1996 that "Ceremonies that celebrate homosexual unions shall not be conducted by our ministers and shall not be conducted in our churches" (*The Book of Discipline*, 87). At the same time, fifteen United Methodist bishops, in a remarkable prophetic action, issued a statement during that conclave, "breaking the silence" and expressing their pain over their "personal convictions that are contradicted by the proscriptions in the *Discipline* against gay and lesbian persons within our

church and within our ordained and diaconal ministers" and urging "our United Methodist churches to open the doors in gracious hospitality to all our brothers and sisters in the faith."

5. George Anderson, "Pastor Suggests Sophia Article Included Heresy," *United Methodist Connection*, 9 March 1994, A-5.

12. Exorcising the Social Demons

1. James Bitney and Yvette Nelson, eds., *Welcome to the Way: A Confirmation Catechesis* (Allen, Tex.: Tabor Publishing, 1989), 60.

2. William R. Macklin, "Breaking a Cardinal Rule," *Philadelphia Enquirer*, 8 October 1993. This account is based on Macklin's article.

Selected Bibliography

Barth, Karl. *Church Dogmatics*, vol. 4, part 4 (Grand Rapids: William B. Eerdmans Publishing Co., 1981).

Baum, Gregory, ed. *Religion and Alienation: A Theological Reading of Sociology* (New York: Paulist Press, 1976).

—————. *Theology and Society* (New York: Paulist Press, 1988).

Boff, Leonardo. *The Lord's Prayer: The Prayer of Integral Liberation* (Maryknoll, N.Y.: Orbis Books, 1983).

Bonhoeffer, Dietrich. *Life Together: A Discussion of Christian Fellowship*, reprint ed. (San Francisco: HarperCollins, 1992).

Casaldáliga, Pedro and Vigil, José-María. *Political Holiness: A Spirituality of Liberation*, trans. Burns, Paul, and McDonagh (Maryknoll, N.Y.: Orbis Books, 1994).

Clark, Linda, Marian Ronan, and Eleanor Walker. *Image-breaking/Image-building: A Handbook for Creative Worship with Women of Christian Tradition* (New York: Pilgrim Press, 1981).

Clarke, Corita. *A Spirituality for Active Ministry* (Kansas City: Sheed and Ward, 1991).

Crosby, Michael H. *Thy Will Be Done: Praying the Our Father as a Subversive Activity* (Maryknoll, N.Y.: Orbis Books, 1977).

Del Bene, Ron. *The Breath of Life—A Simple Way to Pray* (Nashville: Upper Room Books, 1992).

Edwards, Tilden H. *Living in the Presence: Disciplines for the Spiritual Heart* (San Francisco: Harper & Row, 1987).

—————. *Living with Apocalypse: Spiritual Resources for Social Compassion* (San Francisco: Harper & Row, 1984).

—————. *Spiritual Friend: Reclaiming the Gift of Spiritual Direction* (New York: Paulist Press, 1980).

Elliott, Charles. *Praying the Kingdom: Towards a Political Spirituality* (New York: Paulist Press, 1985).

Finger, Thomas N. *Christian Theology: An Eschatological Approach*, vol. I (Scottsdale, Penn.: Herald Press, 1987).

Fitzgerald, Constance, O.C.D. "Impasse and Dark Night." In Tilden H. Edwards, ed., *Living with Apocalypse: Spiritual Resources for Social Compassion*, 93-116 (San Francisco: Harper & Row, 1984).

Gottwald, Norman K. *The Hebrew Bible—A Socio-Literary Introduction* (Philadelphia: Fortress Press, 1985).

————. *The Hebrew Bible in Its Social World and in Ours* (Atlanta: Scholars Press, 1993).

Haughey, John C., ed. *The Faith That Does Justice: Examining the Christian Sources for Social Change* (New York: Paulist Press, 1977).

Hessel, Dieter T. *Social Ministry*, rev. ed. (Louisville: Westminster/John Knox Press, 1992).

Hinkelammert, Franz J. *The Ideological Weapons of Death: A Theological Critique of Capitalism* (Maryknoll, N.Y.: Orbis Books, 1986).

Holland, Joe, and Henriot, Peter. *Social Analysis: Linking Faith and Justice* (Maryknoll, N.Y.: Orbis Books, 1983).

Jones, W. Paul. *Trumpet at Full Moon: An Introduction to Christian Spirituality as Diverse Practice* (Louisville, Ky.: Westminster/John Knox Press, 1992).

Kavanaugh, John F. *Still Following Christ in a Consumer Society: The Spirituality of Cultural Resistance* (Maryknoll, N.Y.: Orbis Books, 1991).

Keating, Thomas. *Open Mind, Open Heart: The Contemplative Dimension of the Gospel*, rev. ed. (New York: Continuum, 1994).

————. *Intimacy with God* (New York: Crossroad, 1994).

Kellerman, Bill Wylie. *Seasons of Faith and Conscience: Kairos, Confession, Liturgy* (Maryknoll, N.Y.: Orbis, 1991).

Kelly, Thomas R. *A Testament of Devotion*, reprint ed. (San Francisco: Harper SF, 1992).

Koenig, John. *Rediscovering New Testament Prayer: Boldness and Blessing in the Name of Jesus* (New York: HarperCollins, 1992).

Leech, Kenneth. *True Prayer: An Invitation to Christian Spirituality* (San Francisco: Harper SF, 1986).

————. *The Eye of the Storm: Living Spirituality in the Real World* (New York: HarperCollins, 1992).

Magdoff, Harry and Paul M. Sweeney. "Marxism and Religion." In William K. Tabb, *Churches in Struggle: Liberation Theologies and Social Change in North America* (New York: Monthly Review Press, 1986).

May, Gerald G. *The Awakened Heart: Living Beyond Addiction* (San Francisco: Harper SF, 1993).

———. *Will and Spirit: A Contemplative Psychology* (San Francisco: Harper SF, 1987).

Morris, Danny E. *Yearning to Know God's Will: A Workbook for Discovering God's Guidance for Your Life* (Grand Rapids: Zondervan, 1991).

Mosala, Itumeleng J. *Biblical Hermeneutics and Black Theology in South Africa* (Grand Rapids: William B. Eerdmans Publishing Co., 1989).

Norberg, Tilda, and Webber, Robert D. *Stretch Out Your Hand: Exploring Healing Prayer* (Cleveland: United Church Press, 1990). This title is currently out of print but is being reissued by Upper Room Books.

Olsen, Charles M. *Transforming Church Boards into Communities of Spiritual Leaders* (Bethesda, Md.: The Alban Institute, 1995).

Peacock, Larry J. *Heart and Soul: A Guide for Spiritual Formation in the Local Church* (Nashville: The Upper Room, 1992).

Peterson, Robin and Lou Ann Parsons. *See-Judge-Act: Pastoral Planning for a Prophetic Church* (Cleveland: United Church Board for World Ministries, 1991).

Pleins, J. David. *The Psalms: Songs of Tragedy, Hope, and Justice* (Maryknoll, N.Y.: Orbis Books, 1993).

Roemer, Sister Judith, A.N.G. *The Group Meeting as a Contemplative Experience* (Wernersville, Penn.: Typrofile Press, 1983).

Ruth, Nancy. *The Breath of God: An Approach to Prayer* (Cambridge, Mass.: Cowley Publications, 1990).

Schneiders, Sandra M. *The Revelatory Text: Interpreting the New Testament as Sacred Scripture* (New York: HarperCollins, 1991).

Schüssler-Fiorenza, Elisabeth. *In Memory of Her: A Feminist Theological Reconstruction of Christian Origins* (New York: Crossroad, 1983).

Steere, Douglas V. *Dimensions of Prayer* (Nashville: Upper Room Books, 1997).

Tillich, Paul. *The Political Expectation*, ed. James Luther Adams (Lanham, Md.: University Press of America, 1983).

The System Belongs to God. UMCom Productions, a series of seven videotapes available from EcuFilm, Nashville, Tenn., (800-251-4091).

Wagley, Laurence A. "Prayer for the Hurried, the Undisciplined and the Disorganized." *Christian Century* 110 (24-31 March, 1993), 323-5.

Weber, Joseph. "Christ's Victory Over the Powers." In *Above Every Name: The Lordship of Christ and Social Systems*, 66-82, ed. Thomas E. Clark (Ramsey, N.J.: Paulist Press, 1980).

West, Cornel. *Prophesy Deliverance: An Afro-American Revolutionary Christianity* (Philadelphia: Westminster Press, 1982).

Wingeier, Douglas E. "Discernment as a Mode of Church Planning." *Circuit Rider*, September 1984, 4-5.

Wink, Walter. *Naming the Powers: The Language of Power in the New Testament*, series 1 (Philadelphia: Fortress Press, 1984).

─────. *Unmasking the Powers: The Invisible Forces That Determine Human Existence*, series 2 (Philadelphia: Fortress Press, 1993).

─────. *Engaging the Powers: Discernment and Resistance in a World of Domination*, series 3 (Philadelphia: Fortress Press, 1992).

Index